SHARING STITCHES

one-of-a-kind
projects
to sew and su

Chrissie Grace

NORTH
LIGHT
BOOKS

CINCINNATI, OHIO

DIRECT

E BY F+W INTERNATIONAL
12 4PU, England
Tel: (+44) 1626 323200, Fax: (   ) 26 323319
E-mail: postmaster@davidandcharles.co.uk

DISTRIBUTED IN AUSTRALIA BY CAPRICORN LINK
P.O. Box 704, S. Windsor NSW, 2756 Australia
Tel: (02) 4577-3555

Library of Congress Cataloging-in-Publication Data
Grace, Chrissie.
  Sharing stitches : one-of-a-kind projects to sew and swap / Chrissie Grace. -- 1st ed.
    p. cm.
  Includes index.
  ISBN-13: 978-1-60061-943-4 (pbk. : alk. paper)
  1. Sewing. I. Title.
TT705.G73 2010
  746--dc22

2010030104

fw
media
www.fwmedia.com

Editor Rachel Scheller

Designer Julie Barnett

Production Coordinator Greg Nock

Photographer Christine Polomsky

Stylist Jan Nickum

Metric Conversion Chart

TO CONVERT	TO	MULTIPLY BY
inches	centimeters	2.54
centimeters	inches	0.4
feet	centimeters	30.5
centimeters	feet	0.03
yards	meters	0.9
meters	yards	1.1

ACKNOWLEDGMENTS

I would like to thank Tonia Davenport and North Light Books for choosing me to become a third-time author for them. Many thanks to my editor Rachel Scheller for navigating with me through this journey and for her limitless patience. Christine Polomsky, whom I was lucky enough to work with again, thank you for your amazing photography skills and generosity in the studio. Finally, a shout out to Julie Barnett for your wonderful design. Thanks, everyone!

DEDICATION

I have been blessed my whole life with wonderful girlfriends. Girlfriends who I've known since elementary school. Girlfriends who laughed with me in middle school, cried with me in high school, and watched me get married and have children. These women have been a rock in my life, and I don't know what I would do without them!

I was blessed again to form friendships with the women who contributed to this book. This book would be nothing without the talent and commitment from the contributors. Thank you to every artist who participated in the swaps and collaborations that we did. I learned so much from you, and I'm so glad to share your work for many others to see.

This book is dedicated to all the wonderful women whom I have been honored to call friends.

contents

Introduction

Perhaps you are an accomplished sewer who would like to learn more about altering fabric into mixed-media art pieces. Maybe you are a prolific artist who would like to learn how to use a sewing machine to incorporate fabric pieces into your work. You might just have an intense desire to quilt, sew or create things with fabric. If any of these descriptions apply to you, then you have picked up the right book.

I consider myself a mixed-media artist. I have a long past creating mosaic art with glass and tile. I also love to paint and create mixed-media collages. Working as an artist has always been a solitary experience for me. Whether it was in my garage studio, at my kitchen table or alone in my car jotting down ideas, my artistic dialogue was limited to myself. I started yearning for a connection to other artists. I wanted to connect to some creative partners with whom I could develop a small artistic community. It wasn't until I made the decision to step outside my little work zone in my home studio that I really started blossoming.

A few years ago I wanted to learn how to sew and took a quilting class at a local sewing studio. I hit many roadblocks along the way trying to figure things out on my own. Let's just say that my seam ripper and I became very close! Creating my blog (www.chrissiegrace.blogspot.com) led me to develop relationships with other artists and sewers who were happily offering tutorials online. I saw that quilters were having online quilting swaps and a lot of painters were hosting round robin journal collaborations. After joining and completing a few of these swaps and collaborations, I realized how much I was learning! Working with other artists can provide you with

knowledge and inspiration that is impossible to gain by working alone. Besides that, it's just plain fun!

When I created this book, I wanted to host a number of online swaps and collaborations focusing on fabric art. I have an affinity for both functioning fabric pieces (quilts, home accessory items and garments) and fabric art (altered fabric art pieces, fabric round robin journals and quilt blocks) for their aesthetic qualities. I decided to include a mix of both types of projects in the book.

I wanted to represent an eclectic group of sewers and artists, so I asked people with very different backgrounds to participate. Some of the people in our group were very experienced sewers, while others didn't know how to sew but had the desire to learn. They actually learned through the process of our projects! You will find that if you decide to host a collaboration or swapping group, you will have participants who range in levels from beginner to advanced. Be prepared to work with people of all technical levels. This is part of the fun; when you are in a group, you are both learning and teaching at the same time.

If you are trying to decide whether you would like to either participate in or host a swap or collaboration, consider the power of working with a group. When you participate, the projects are usually assigned a theme. This theme may be a subject that you would not normally choose to work with. Your imagination will be stretched as you wrap your creative senses around that subject. Knowing that other people are collaborating with you gives you a sense of artistic security. There is an unspoken agreement that while you are working with other people, you are giving the same precious time and respect that other artists are giving.

One aspect of collaborations and swapping to be aware of is deadlines. Some artists or sewers are

intimidated by deadlines. They don't want their work to feel rushed. But deadlines are a great way to hone your artistic processes. Sometimes, it is good to just go with your first idea, and if you are a perfectionist, to let it go when it's time. You also need to be respectful of deadlines for other people's sake. There is nothing more disappointing to fellow participants than when someone makes a commitment and then is late or backs out. Of course, unexpected events come up, but always try to communicate clearly with your host if you are having a hard time keeping up.

The most exciting part of collaborating with others is the inspiration you gain. Your take on a subject will be completely and totally different than someone else's. When we completed the round robin project for this book and I got it back in the mail, I was in tears over the talent encompassed in that package. While the thirteen artists had been given the same theme, they all had expressed a different interpreta-

tion. Knowing that it had taken almost nine months to complete and had traveled all over the country was an overwhelming feeling. It was so exciting to hold all that inspiration in my hands! I really felt connected to all the other participants at that point.

When participating in projects, there are many online sites where you can post pictures of the projects in process, as well as the finished art. I consider this to be an essential part of the process, so that everyone can see the fruits of each other's labors and be recognized for their part in the finished product.

I hope you are inspired by the efforts of *Sharing Stitches*. I had so much fun writing it, and I am honored by the women who chose to participate. Thank you, ladies, for your time and effort, and for the many lessons you taught me along the way.

SWAPPING and COLLABORATING

SWAPPING

When swapping, I suggest starting small. Do a swap with one person. Agree to send each other a box of items to work with (keep it under $20) and then see what each one of you creates. Do another one with three to five people. Everyone can send a fabric to each participant and receive just as many various fabrics in return. As your participant list grows, your variation in fabrics gets larger, too.

I recently did a quilting swap where we made one hundred quilt blocks. The theme was simply red and aqua. I sent my blocks to the host, and I received one hundred different blocks from the other ninety-nine participants. I now have a huge range of blocks to make a quilt with. This swap was a lot of work, but it was so much fun!

COLLABORATING

There are so many online groups available that it can be quite overwhelming to pick one to join. One of the best places to start is a Yahoo group (http://groups.yahoo.com). Try to narrow your search by typing in keywords such as *sewing* or *round robin*. If you can't find a group that matches your interest, think about creating your own. Being active on a personal blog can help you connect with people who may be interested in participating.

When you are part of a collaboration, there may be questions about who gets to keep the final product. With some groups, you will agree to do enough collaborative pieces that everyone in the group will get to keep one. Sometimes (as in the case for the two collaborations we did in this book), you can auction the piece off and use the proceeds to donate to a charity. This is a great way to give back to the community. Make sure everyone in the group is clear about the resulting piece's destiny.

 Collaborating Online

If you are looking for an online group to join, here are some places to start:

- http://groups.yahoo.com
- www.ebsquart.com
- www.sewing365.com
- http://quiltwithus.connectingthreads.com
- www.artellawordsandart.com
- http://quiltinggallery.com/press/the-virtual-quilting-bee

ETIQUETTE

When swapping and/or collaborating, remember these online group etiquette tips:

- Each host sets forth the guidelines for the swap. These guidelines are not negotiable. Read them several times before joining the swap. E-mail the host for clarification before joining if any part of the guidelines is confusing to you.

- Be careful not to overextend yourself on swaps! Also, be sure to know the mailing date of your swap. Notify the host right away if you are going to be late sending in your contributions.

- If the host states that fabric should be quilt shop quality, do everyone a favor and send fabric from your local/online quilt shop. It may be tempting to pay $3 a yard for something that's on sale, but it isn't really fair to those who have paid for a more expensive fabric. This rule goes for any swapped materials.

- It is imperative that your packages be sent to the host with adequate postage. Be sure not only that you include a self-addressed return envelope, but also that you put the correct stamped postage on the return envelope.

- Sending your host a small gift is always appreciated, although it is not required. The host has done a lot of organization and work to make the project a success. Extra fabric or sewing supplies make great gifts, or even just a nice thank-you note will suffice.

Getting Involved

This book focuses on swaps and collaborations conceived via the Internet. If you are fortunate enough to be involved in a local art community where you live, keep in mind that all of these projects can be done in sewing guilds or groups. Check your local sewing stores to see if they have formed any collaborative groups. If not, perhaps you can be the facilitator! I have not had the opportunity yet to be part of a local collaborating group, but I can only imagine that it would deepen the connections made.

MATERIALS *and* TOOLS

Whenever embarking on a new journey, you want to be prepared. Fabric art materials and tools encompass a large spectrum, and you will use a variety of both sewing and art supplies. It is nice to have a specific work area, such as a sewing table, with all your supplies nicely organized. If space is an issue, you can always use your kitchen table and keep your supplies in a rolling cart that can be stored elsewhere. Either way, it is helpful to have your materials and tools easily accessible, so you don't waste your time running around looking for what you need. Included in this section are some of the items you will use frequently for the projects in this book.

FABRIC

Muslin fabric is used frequently in the projects in this book. It is a very inexpensive and easy material to work with. You will also use a large variety of quilting fabrics, which are normally 100-percent cotton. Use caution when shopping for fabrics, because it can become addictive and quite expensive! There are so many beautiful fabrics available in sewing shops, online or in craft stores. You can experiment with many different fabrics, such as velvets, silks and rayons, as you gain more sewing experience.

FABRIC ADHESIVES

I use several different fabric adhesives, and they all have different properties.

- White glue: Use white glue or a glue stick as a fabric adhesive. It will temporarily hold fabric until it is sewn, so you don't have to pin it. People will often use this when sewing thick fabrics, such as felt.

- Spray fabric adhesive: This is convenient because it is not messy or sticky to use. It comes in a spray can, but you must use it in a well-ventilated area, because it does contain toxic fumes.

- Fabric glue: A permanent fabric glue is great for attaching gems and rhinestones to items that will be laundered. A nonwashable version can be used for decorative fabric art.

- Fusible web: Fusible web, or bonding fabric, is a layer of adhesive material that is placed between two layers of fabric to fuse them together permanently.

- Fusible interfacing: Fusible interfacing includes fabric adhesive already bonded to a material.

NEEDLES

When you are doing embroidery, it is important to have the correct needle. When using standard embroidery thread, which is available at any craft store, the best needle to use is a size 9 or 10 needle. They both work well with linen or cotton fabrics. If you will be adding beads to your embroidery, you will need to use a beading needle, which is extra long and thin to accommodate a large amount of beads.

PAINTING SUPPLIES

When you are creating mixed-media fiber art, canvas is a great medium for both painting and sewing. You can purchase canvas pads with pre-cut pieces in various sizes. Claudine Hellmuth sells a very inventive product called Sticky-Back Canvas. It is the same as regular canvas, except that the back peels off and you can stick it onto other surfaces. You will also need a variety of inexpensive acrylic paints along with some paintbrushes, which are available at any craft store. If you will be laundering the piece, it is advisable to invest in some fabric paints.

ROTARY CUTTER, MAT AND TRANSPARENT RULER

Be careful when using your rotary cutter. When it's not in use, make sure to slide it down and lock it because it is very sharp and could cause a deep cut. When your fabric is not cutting like butter anymore, it's time to replace the blade.

Rotary mats protect your work surface when cutting fabric and other materials. They are also made of a material that keeps your rotary cutter blade sharp. I suggest purchasing a 24"× 36" (61cm × 91.5cm) mat if possible. You will also need a transparent ruler, which is used to measure, grip and accurately cut pieces of fabric.

SCISSORS

You will need a few pairs of scissors for the projects in this book: a tiny set for snipping threads and a pair of fabric scissors reserved for cutting fabric. If you need to cut paper, you will need a third pair of scissors; don't use your fabric scissors, as cutting paper will dull the blades. It is also handy to have a pair of pinking shears.

SEAM RIPPER

Whether you are a beginning sewer or advanced, you will certainly benefit from a seam ripper. It makes pulling the stitches out of your mistakes much easier.

SEWING MACHINE

If you are a seasoned sewer, you probably already own a machine. However, if you are a beginner, there are many things to consider before buying a sewing machine. Of all your sewing tools, it is surely the largest investment. If you are a beginner, I suggest buying a less expensive machine and making sure that sewing is something that you love! When you do purchase your sewing machine, read the instruction guide front to back. Learn all the names of the parts of the sewing machine and gain a general knowledge as to what each part does. Do a lot of practicing. Try to find a local class on basic sewing so you can get comfortable using your machine. Find a friend or family member who is not only experienced but patient, too!

SEWING NOTIONS

You will need straight pins and an iron and ironing board to complete the projects in this book.

THREAD

When you go into the sewing or craft store to buy thread for your machine, you may be overwhelmed by the large selection. For all of the projects we create in this book, an all-purpose thread will suffice. A general piecing thread can be used in all machines and basically works for most projects. Don't use any old thread that you may have lying around. If you pull the thread off the spool and it breaks, it will break in your machine. Go ahead and throw it away. Also, when you put the thread on your machine, be sure that you place the top part of the spool up. If you hold the spool horizontally by the top and bottom, your thread should hang freely. If you put it in the wrong way, your thread will catch on itself.

Some projects in this book call for hand-embroidery. Embroidery thread has six strands of thread. You can use all six strands for a thicker embroidery line, or remove some of them to vary the thickness.

TECHNIQUES

FREEZER PAPER METHOD

For some of your projects you will want to print an image or words on fabric. Instead of buying transfer paper and ironing it on, you can make your own fabric paper. Cut a piece of freezer paper and a piece of muslin a little larger than a standard 8½" × 11" (21.5cm × 28cm) page. Place the plastic side of the freezer paper down on your muslin and iron them together. The two pieces will become one. Make sure to trim it to 8½" × 11" (21.5cm × 28cm) with no hanging strings. You can now feed it right into your ink-jet printer. Make sure that the image will print on the fabric side of the paper.

IRONING

It is imperative that you press all of your fabric pieces before using them in your projects (unless, of course, the project calls for a wrinkled look!). Ironing your fabric makes everything look more finished, and it's a good habit to get into if you start quilting.

MAKING A MICROWAVE FLOWER PRESS

You can buy a commercial flower press at most craft stores, or you can make your own for practically free.

Cut two pieces of thick cardboard 10" (25.5cm) square, or smaller if your microwave won't accommodate this size. Cut sheets of newsprint in the same size. Place a piece of newsprint on one piece of cardboard, and then arrange the flowers on top of the newsprint. Lay another piece of newsprint on top of the flowers, and then cover with the other piece of cardboard. Secure with rubber bands around all the edges.

"Cook" the flowers on medium heat (50-percent) for about two minutes. Carefully check them. If they don't seem completely dry, put them back in for another minute or so. When you remove them from the microwave, place them in between a stack of heavy books overnight. The next morning you will have pressed, dried flowers.

STITCHING IN THE DITCH

Stitching in the ditch is a great technique for beginning machine quilters. The term "stitch in the ditch" means that you use the walking foot on your machine to create straight lines of quilting along the seams (or "ditches") of the quilt top. If you are using the stitch-in-the-ditch technique, you must keep your stitches in the seams, or ditches, consistently. You don't want your stitches to veer away from the seams.

STRAIGHT STITCHING

A straight stitch is simply that. Unless otherwise noted, always use a ¼" (6mm) seam.

TOPSTITCHING

Topstitching is a length of stitching done on the top of a seam to give it a finished appearance.

EMBROIDERY STITCHES

Follow the stitch illustrations to bring the needle up at odd numbers and down at even numbers.

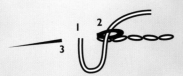

BACKSTITCH

Backstitching resembles a row of machine stitching. Aim for a line of small, evenly sized stitches.

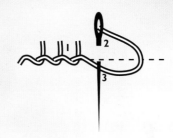

BLANKET STITCH

The blanket stitch is a decorative stitch that finishes a raw edge. Work the stitches evenly and as closely together as necessary to cover the raw edge.

CROSS STITCH

The cross stitch is a decorative stitch made of two stitches that cross each other to make an X.

FRENCH KNOT

A french knot is a compact raised stitch that resembles a bead lying on its side.

RUNNING STITCH

A running stitch is made by running the needle and thread in and out of the fabric to create a simple and versatile line stitch. The running stitch has spaces between each stitch that are equal to the length of the stitches.

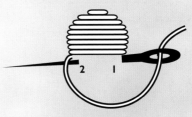

SATIN STITCH

The satin stitching is a filling stitch used to create a smooth surface decoration. It is made up of simple straight stitches laid close together in parallel lines to create a solid filling.

Chapter 1

SPARE A SQUARE

The premise of the "Spare a Square" swap is to trade fabrics with a number of people, and then see what each participant creates using the same fabrics. For the swap featured in this chapter, I asked each of the seven participants to mail me 1 yard (1m) of fabric. For variety's sake, I requested that each person send a different color. When I received the yards of fabric, I cut each yard into seven equal pieces. I made a package for each participant that contained one piece of each fabric. Each person then created their own project.

When hosting one of these swaps through the Internet, it's a good idea to set up an online photo gallery on a website such as Flickr (www.flickr.com) so all the participants can upload their individual projects when they are finished. It is really exciting to see what everyone has created! Another advantage of uploading to an online photo gallery is that everyone can leave comments for each other. If you are part of a local swap group that will meet in person, I suggest having a "reveal" party where everyone brings their finished projects. Everyone will have the chance to see the shared fabrics in person.

This type of swap can be varied in so many different ways. One of the things I love most about this swap is that you can do it with as few as three people, and there is no limit to how many people could sign up. When you have a small group, it is easier to be specific about color or print requests. If it grows to be a larger swap, where you may have as many as one hundred participants, you could do a scrap swap. Participants could send five to ten scraps and receive five to ten different scraps from a different swap participant. Just keep in mind that, when hosting these larger swaps, you are in for more work! Also, remember to be firm with deadlines and always request that the participants send a self-addressed envelope with adequate postage.

Have fun with the Spare a Square swap. It is very exciting in the end to see what everyone creates!

PATCHWORK PULLOVER

Designed by Sara Mincy

I have always been attracted to Sara Mincy's style; her paintings are bold, colorful and simple. When I contacted her about participating in the swap, she informed me that she was a beginning sewer. "That's perfect!" I told her. When you are participating in swaps, you will sometimes find a vast difference in people's experience levels. Some people will be seasoned sewers, while others will still be learning how to use their machines. This shirt is a great project for beginners, though it is still fun for those of you who have been sewing for a long time. The patchwork lends itself to different types of person-alities. Some will like the squares and rectangles to be perfectly geometric and will prefer the fabrics to appear in a pattern. Others might cut shapes randomly and not want any sense of order to the fabrics. Variations to this project could include adding buttons to the centers of the shapes, cutting the fabrics into different shapes such as circles or ovals, and extending the length of the design to cover the entire shirt.

materials

100-percent cotton T-shirt

fabric from swap

fabric in coordinating colors (optional)

fusible web

sewing thread

Note: To complete the project, the swap fabrics should total at least 1 yard (1m).

tools

iron and ironing board

rotary cutter and mat

scissors

sewing machine

transparent ruler

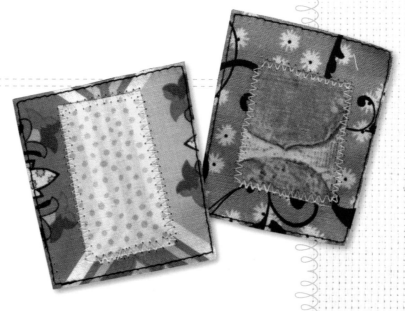

1 Using a rotary cutter, mat and transparent ruler, cut a 2" × 5" (5cm × 12.5cm) rectangle of fusible web. Place the fusible web under a piece of swap fabric. The adhesive side of the fusible web should be facing the wrong side of the fabric.

2 Iron the fabric to the fusible web following the manufacturer's instructions.

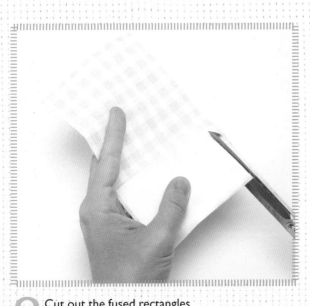

3 Cut out the fused rectangles.

4 Peel off the fusible web paper to reveal the adhesive. Repeat Steps 1–4 to make 12 large rectangles in various fabrics. You may choose to use additional coordinating fabrics to complete some of the rectangles.

5 Arrange the large squares on the front of a T-shirt in 3 rows of 4 squares. A 100-percent cotton T-shirt is best.

6 Fuse the large squares to the shirt with an iron.

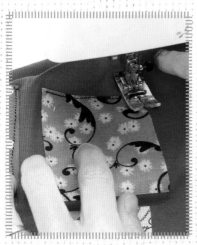

7 Sew a straight stitch around each large rectangle.

8 Refer to Steps 1–4 to fuse and cut 12 1" × 3" (2.5cm × 7.5cm) rectangles from swap or coordinating fabrics. Arrange the smaller rectangles over the larger rectangles and fuse them in place with an iron.

9 Stitch around the smaller rectangles using a zigzag stitch.

NO PLACE LIKE HOME DISHCLOTH

Designed by Catherine Thursby

One trait of fascinating artists is their ability to make ordinary items unique and special. Catherine Thursby has a whimsical and eclectic style that lends itself well to making functional items uniquely funky. Using the fabrics from the swap, she turned an everyday dishcloth into a miniature piece of art for the kitchen. There are endless variations of this project that would be great to use as kitchen accessories in your own home or for gift-giving. How about appliquéing some fruit and vegetables, an assortment of frosted cupcakes or a variety of kitchen appliances onto a towel or apron? This technique would serve well for creating special hand towels in the bathroom, too. A yellow bath duck with bubbles, a beach theme, or the recipient's name or initials are just a few appliquéing ideas. Or use your imagination to create one-of-a-kind curtains, pillowcases or even seat covers.

materials

100-percent cotton dishtowel, at least 18" (45.5cm) wide

fabric from swap

fabric in coordinating colors

fusible web

sewing thread

Note: To complete the project, the swap fabrics should total at least 1 yard (1m).

tools

iron and ironing board

pencil

rotary cutter and mat

scissors

sewing machine

straight pins

templates for door, roof and lettering (see page 132)

transparent ruler

1 Copy the provided template letters *H, O, M* and *E* and cut them out.

2 Sew together strips of swap fabric in varying widths. The resulting striped fabric should be at least 4" × 15" (10cm × 38cm). Iron the striped fabric onto fusible web.

3 Pin the letters onto the striped fabric and cut them out.

4 Iron the letters onto the shorter edge of a 100-percent cotton dishtowel.

5 Outline each letter with a satin stitch.

6 Sew together strips of swap fabric for the roof piece and iron the fabric onto fusible web. Pin or trace the roof template onto the striped fabric and cut out the roof shape.

7 Cut a 4" × 6¾" (10cm × 17cm) rectangle of coordinating fabric for the house piece and iron it onto fusible web.

8 Iron a small piece of coordinating fabric to fusible web. Pin or trace the door template onto this fabric and cut out the door shape.

9 Lay the house and roof pieces above the lettering and fuse them in place with an iron. Fuse the door to the house.

10 Lightly sketch windows on the house with a pencil. Use a satin stitch to outline the window shapes. Satin stitch around the roof, house and door.

WINGS HEAL.

HEARTS MEND.

LIFE MOVES ON.

- Calcium
- Vitamines
  A-D₃-E-C

SCRAPPY BIRD

Designed by Chrissie Grace

When I received my fabrics from the swap, I envisioned making something purely for fun. Birds are a theme that I constantly revisit, and I have recently been using some anthropomorphic images in my work, so I gave this bird a human trait by applying the image of the human eye. I also enjoy the juxtaposition of fabric and natural elements, so I searched for twigs that resembled legs. I think this is a really fun project that could be expanded upon in many ways. What about making a whole family of birds to represent the members of your family? Take a picture of each person's eyes and use them to embellish the birds. You could also make mini birds to serve as ornaments or decorative accents to be hung in various places in your house. Another variation would be to make the bird really large. Instead of using batting, you could stuff it with fiberfill and create an unusual wall hanging.

materials

batting

fabric from swap

fabric glue

fabric paper

fiberfill

freezer paper (optional; for freezer paper method)

fusible web

muslin (optional; for freezer paper method)

sewing thread

2 small branches

Note: To complete the project, the swap fabrics should total at least 1 yard (1m).

tools

hot glue gun and glue sticks

ink-jet printer

iron and ironing board

pencil

rotary cutter and mat

scissors

sewing machine

straight pins

templates for bird body, beak and heart (see page 132)

1 Pin or trace the bird body template onto a piece of fusible web and cut out the bird shape. Repeat this step with a piece of swap fabric and a piece of batting.

2 Print out the image of an eye and a phrase onto fabric paper or use the freezer paper method (see page 12). Cut out the eye and phrase.

25

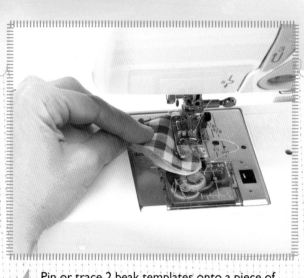

3 Iron a piece of swap fabric onto fusible web. Cut a wing shape from the fabric. I used the design on the fabric to guide my wing shape. You can also draw your own wing or print a wing shape onto fabric paper. I cut out circles from this same fabric design to adhere to the body of the bird. Iron another piece of fusible web to another piece of swap fabric and cut out a piece for head feathers.

4 Pin or trace 2 beak templates onto a piece of swap fabric and cut them out. Make a sandwich with a small amount of fiberfill between the 2 fabric beaks. Straight stitch all the way around. Repeat this process to create a stuffed heart, using the heart template and another piece of swap fabric.

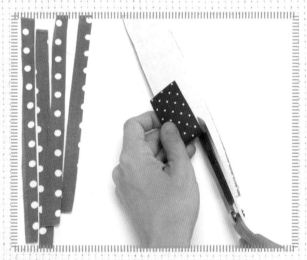

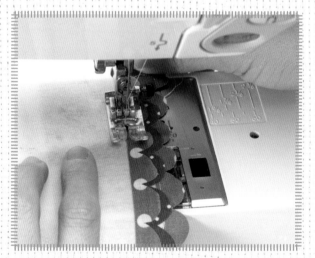

5 Iron a 7" (18cm) square of swap fabric onto fusible web. Cut the fabric into 7 strips measuring ½" × 7" (1.5cm × 18cm). Repeat this process with a different swap fabric.

6 Draw a scallop shape onto the fusible web side of each strip with a pencil. Cut along the lines. Starting at the bottom of the fusible web bird piece from Step 1, iron a strip onto the body, then sew across it using a straight stitch. Repeat this process for all the strips, alternating the 2 different colors and overlapping the strips slightly. Trim the edges all the way around the body to maintain the bird shape.

7 Sew the phrase from Step 2 onto a piece of swap fabric. Cut it into several pieces and sew each piece onto the bird's belly with a decorative stitch. Repeat this process for attaching the eye image.

8 Make a fabric hook by cutting 2 strips of fabric measuring 2" × 4" (5cm × 10cm). Sandwich a slightly smaller piece of batting between the 2 strips and sew all the way around. Fold the strip in half to make a loop and pin it to the fabric bird piece from Step 1. Straight stitch across the bottom of the loop.

9 Sandwich the batting bird piece between the fabric bird piece and the front bird piece with the scalloped strips. Pin the beak and wing so they lay in the middle of the sandwich. Straight stitch all the way around the bird and remove the pins.

10 Using hot glue, adhere 2 small branches to the bottom of the bird for legs. Using fabric glue, adhere the heart to the bird's chest.

FOLK ART PILLOW

Designed by Sandy Mastroni

Sandy Mastroni is a self-taught artist, and her stylized paint-ings of animals and people are very charming. In this project, Sandy has taken a pillow and turned it into a piece of folk art. When you make this pillow, you have the freedom to paint any-thing you want. Even if you aren't comfortable painting your central image, you can print any copyright-free image onto fabric paper to use as your main image. The front of the pillow can be pieced in many different ways. Another technique that Sandy uses in many of her pillows is embellishing with vintage lace, buttons and frayed fabrics. You could sew other variations of this pillow by differing the size. Make it super small to use as an ornament, or larger to use as the focal point on a living room couch.

materials

acrylic paints

batting

black fine point permanent marker

buttons

copyright-free image (optional)

embroidery thread

fabric from swap

fabric in coordinating colors

fiberfill

freezer paper

graphite paper (optional)

muslin

sewing thread

tracing paper (optional)

Note: To complete the project, the swap fabrics should total at least 1 yard (1m).

tools

hot glue gun and glue sticks

iron and ironing board

paintbrush

pencil

pinking shears

rotary cutter and mat

scissors

sewing machine

sewing needle

straight pins

transparent ruler

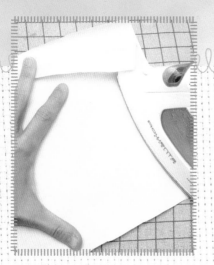  

1 Iron an 8" (20.5cm) square of muslin onto freezer paper using the freezer paper method (see page 12).

2 Draw your own design directly on the muslin, or transfer a copyright-free design onto the muslin using tracing paper and graphite paper.

3 Paint the design using watered-down acrylics, and outline it with a black fine point permanent marker.

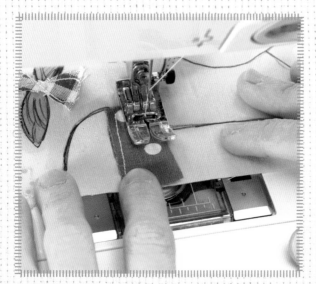 

4 Peel the freezer paper off the back of the muslin. Sew pieces of swap fabric to different elements of the design. You may choose to outline the fabrics with the fine point marker as well. Trim the muslin square on all sides with pinking shears.

5 Sew the muslin square in the center of a 13½" (34.5cm) square of swap fabric. Layer the swap fabric over a 13½" (34.5cm) square of batting and sew together.

6 Stitch triangles of different swap fabrics onto the corners of the 13½" (34.5cm) square of swap fabric. Hand sew a button onto each corner of the muslin square using a needle and embroidery thread.

7 Cut a 13½" (34.5cm) square of coordinating fabric for the pillow backing. With right sides together, stitch the pillow closed completely. Press.

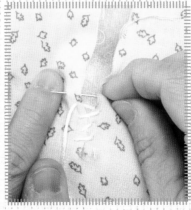

8 Cut a slit in the center of the pillow backing approximately 4" (10cm) long. Turn the pillow right side out through this slit.

9 Stuff the pillow with fiberfill. Hand stitch the back closed.

10 To cover the slit, cut a 2½" × 5" (6.5cm × 12.5cm) piece of coordinating fabric and layer it over a piece of batting cut to the same size. Sew the layers together and trim the piece with pinking shears. Sew a button in the center. Use a hot glue gun to glue the piece over the hand-stitched opening.

LIST LOVER'S NOTEPAD COVER

Designed by Yetta Miller

I am what you would consider a compulsive list-maker. I make lists constantly . . . everything from grocery lists to gift ideas to ideas for art or sewing projects. I love to have a pad of paper on hand at all times to jot down things I don't want to forget. This quilted notebook cover can be carried along in the car or kept at your desk. If you're like me and thoughts come to you in the middle of the night, keep it on your nightstand for scribbling down thoughts or dreams. Yetta Miller designed this cover to hold a pen as well, making it so convenient!

In my opinion, this project is one of the best gift-giving ideas in the book. A college student who is in the midst of perpetual note taking would love one of these. You could keep a younger child busy in the car or at a doctor's appointment by supplying one of these with a blank pad of paper to draw on. You could also give it to one of your favorite list-making friends!

materials

batting

beads (optional)

button

embroidery thread

fabric from swap

fabric in coordinating colors

legal pad of paper

muslin

satin cord or ribbon

sewing thread

water soluble pen

Note: To complete the project, the swap fabrics should total at least 1 yard (1m).

tools

iron and ironing board

rotary cutter and mat

scissors

sewing machine

sewing needle

straight pins

transparent ruler

1 Complete the outer piece of the journal cover by sewing together 12 fabric strips measuring 2" × 15½" (5cm × 39.5cm) from different swap fabrics. Press the seams as you work. Trim the piece to 15½" × 20½" (39.5cm × 52cm).

2 Pin the following pieces together:

Bottom layer: 15½" × 20½" (39.5cm × 52cm) piece of muslin

Middle layer: 15½" × 20½" (39.5cm × 52cm) piece of batting

Top layer: Striped fabric, right side up

3 Quilt the striped fabric, batting and muslin together using a decorative stitch. If your machine isn't capable of a decorative stitch, use the stitch-in-the-ditch technique (see page 12).

4 To make the pocket, fold a 15½" × 20½" (39.5cm × 52cm) piece of swap fabric in half lengthwise, making it 7¼" × 20½" (18.5cm × 52cm) (wrong sides together). Trim the top to even out the edges. Press, then top stitch along the fold.

5 Cut an 18" (45.5cm) piece of ribbon or cord. Attach beads to the end if desired. Layer all the parts of the journal together:

Bottom layer: 15½" × 20½" (39.5cm × 52cm) piece of coordinating fabric for the lining, right side up

Middle layer: Cord or ribbon, placed 7¼" (18.5cm) down the right edge of the lining; the beaded end of the cord should extend past the right edge of the lining by at least 2½" (6.5cm)

Top layer: Pocket, right side down

6 Place the outer piece of the journal over the pocket, right side down. Pin the layers together, leaving a 2½" (6.5cm) opening for turning.

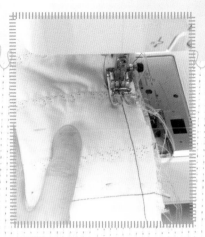

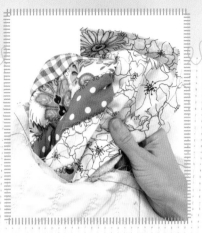

7 Sew all the way around the piece using a ¼" (6mm) seam. Be sure to lock stitches on either side of the opening. Press.

8 Clip the corners, and then turn the journal cover right side out through the opening. Press.

9 Pin together the seam you left open and slip stitch it closed. Top stitch the entire piece. Press.

10 Open the journal cover and insert a legal pad of paper into the right side of the pocket. Draw a line with a water soluble pen, ¼" (6mm) from the left edge of the pad. Remove the pad, and then draw another line 1" (2.5cm) to the left of the first line. Stitch along the lines to create the pen holder.

11 Hand stitch a button on the front of the cover with embroidery thread. Wrap the cord around the button to close.

❀ TIP

You can experiment with the look of the journal cover by quilting it in different ways. Try quilting blocks or a log cabin design.

Keys To A Happy Home

KEYS TO A HAPPY HOME

Designed by Lori Vliegen

In addition to being a fabric and fiber artist, Lori Vliegen is a very talented calligrapher. I love her work for its simplicity, clean lines and impeccable craftsmanship. Every single detail of her art quilt has been crafted with precision and care. Sewing the beads on one by one around the edge of the quilt shows patience and dedication for the work! I love the family theme that the quilt encompasses, with the mixed-media element of the keys amidst the fabric. Although I happen to love the prints she uses, you can certainly use fabrics to fit your personal tastes. Instead of hanging the piece, you could center it in a shadow box. You could also add more personal elements by printing out pictures of family members and sewing them into the background.

materials

anti-fray solution (optional)

buttons

cotton batting

dowel rod or thin branch

embroidery thread

fabric from swap

fabric glue

fabric in coordinating colors

freezer paper

ink pads or colored chalks

3 keys

sewing thread

silver brad shaped like a lock

small glass beads

3 small silver brads

sticky-back canvas (optional)

white cardstock

Note: To complete the project, the swap fabrics should total at least 1 yard (1m). The instructions for this project refer to the different swap fabrics by letters A–J to avoid confusion. Gather 10 different swap and coordinating fabrics and assign each a letter before you begin.

tools

hole punch

ink-jet printer

paintbrush

rotary cutter and mat

scissors

sewing needle

straight pins

transparent ruler

Cutting Guide

Cutting your fabric before beginning the art quilt will save time and help to avoid confusion.

Triangles: Cut to measurements, then cut a scalloped edge into the base of each.

Fabric A:
- 1 rectangle: 4" × 6¼" (10cm × 16cm)
- 3 rectangles: 1¾" × 3½" (4.5cm × 9cm)
- reserved piece for title

Fabric B:
- 1 rectangle: 4½" × 6¾" (11.5cm × 17cm)
- 3 rectangles: 2" × 3⅞" (5cm × 10cm)
- 1 rectangle: 1¾" × 8⅜" (4.5cm × 21.5cm)
- 1 rectangle: 12" × 12½" (30.5cm × 32cm) (backing)
- 1 rectangle: 3" × 7" (7.5cm × 18cm) (hanging loop)

Fabric C: 1 rectangle: 11½" × 12" (29cm × 30.5cm) (backing)

Fabric D: 1 rectangle: 2" × 3¾" (5cm × 9.5cm) (house)

Fabric E: 1 triangle: 2¾" (7cm) along the base (roof)

Fabric F: 1 triangle: 2¾" (7cm) along the base (roof)

Fabric G: 1 triangle: 3" (7.5cm) along the base (roof)

Fabric H: 1 triangle: 3" (7.5cm) along the base (roof)

Fabric I: 1 small heart shape to fit

Fabric J: 2 rectangles: 4" × 5" (10cm × 12.5cm) (tabs at top)

Cotton batting:
- 1 rectangle: 11½" × 12" (29cm × 30.5cm) (backing)
- 1 triangle (to fit behind roof and house)

1 Using the cutting guide to the left, cut fabrics A–J. If desired, place the fabric pieces onto sticky-back canvas to add stability and apply an anti-fray solution around the edges.

2 Print the title *Keys to a Happy Home* onto the reserved piece of fabric A using the freezer paper method (see page 12). Cut the piece to 1½" × 8" (4cm × 20.5cm). If desired, attach the piece to sticky-back canvas. Attach the title to the fabric B rectangle measuring 1¾" × 8⅜" (4.5cm × 21.5cm) with fabric glue, using a paintbrush to spread the glue evenly.

3 Using fabric glue, attach the 4" × 6¼" (10cm × 16cm) fabric A rectangle to the 4½" × 6¾" (11.5cm × 17cm) fabric B rectangle. Attach the 3 fabric A rectangles measuring 1¾" × 3½" (4.5cm × 9cm) to the 3 fabric B rectangles measuring 2" × 3⅞" (5cm × 10cm).

4 Using the schematic on page 41 as a guide, assemble the house using fabrics D–H. Attach a silver brad shaped like a lock to the front of the house piece. Glue the house and roof to the 4" × 6¼" (10cm × 16cm) fabric A rectangle with fabric glue.

✿ TIP

If you want a more handstitched look for your art quilt, you can omit the instructions for using fabric glue and use a straight stitch to secure fabric instead.

5 Sew the fabric I heart and a small button to the roof with embroidery thread, sewing through all the layers.

6 Print words such as *love*, *trust*, *hope* and *family* onto white cardstock and cut them into small tags. Add color to the ends of the tags using ink pads or colored chalks. Punch small holes into the ends of the tags with a hole punch and attach a small silver brad to a group of 2 or 3 tags. Wrap embroidery thread around each brad and tie a group of tags to the top of each key.

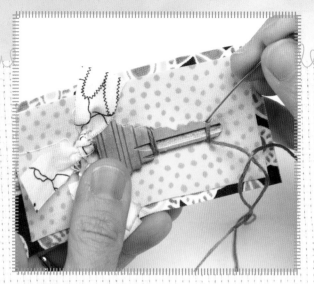

7 Cut 3 narrow strips of fabric J and tie a strip to the top of each key. Sew the keys onto the 1¾" × 3½" (4.5cm × 9cm) fabric A rectangles, using a whipstitch to secure.

8 Assemble the backing by layering the 12" × 12½" (30.5cm × 32cm) fabric B rectangle (right side up) on the bottom, the 11½" × 12" (29cm × 30.5cm) piece of batting in the middle and the 11½" × 12" (29cm × 30.5cm) fabric C rectangle (right side up) on the top.

9 Fold the 3" × 7" (7.5cm × 18cm) fabric B strip in half, wrong sides together, so the piece measures 1½" × 7" (4cm × 18cm). Place it on the wrong side of the backing, at the top, with the folded side facing up to create a loop for hanging.

10 Pin around the edges of the backing to keep all layers in place. Hand sew beads around the edge of fabric C with sewing thread, sewing through all the layers.

11 Attach the key and house rectangles to the quilt backing using fabric glue. Sew decorative stitches, buttons, beads, brads and other embellishments as desired. Place a dowel rod or thin branch through the top loop for hanging.

Fabric B:
3" × 7" (7.5cm × 18cm) folded to 1½" × 7" (4cm × 18cm)

Fabric B:
12" × 12½" (30.5cm × 32cm)

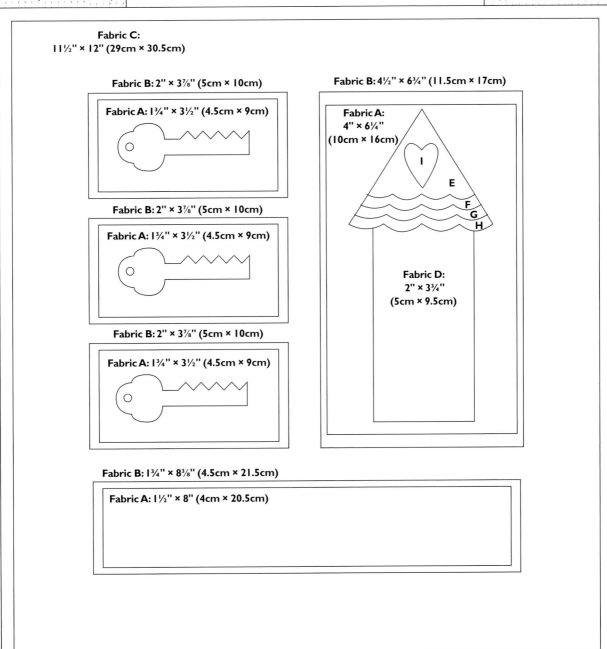

Fabric C:
11½" × 12" (29cm × 30.5cm)

Fabric B: 2" × 3⅞" (5cm × 10cm)

Fabric A: 1¾" × 3½" (4.5cm × 9cm)

Fabric B: 4½" × 6¾" (11.5cm × 17cm)

Fabric A:
4" × 6¼"
(10cm × 16cm)

I

E

F

G

H

Fabric B: 2" × 3⅞" (5cm × 10cm)

Fabric A: 1¾" × 3½" (4.5cm × 9cm)

Fabric D:
2" × 3¾"
(5cm × 9.5cm)

Fabric B: 2" × 3⅞" (5cm × 10cm)

Fabric A: 1¾" × 3½" (4.5cm × 9cm)

Fabric B: 1¾" × 8⅜" (4.5cm × 21.5cm)

Fabric A: 1½" × 8" (4cm × 20.5cm)

AMAZING ARTIST'S APRON

Designed by Liz Lamoreux

Aprons have long been considered a utilitarian item deemed necessary for any successful cook in the kitchen. Liz Lamoreux has taken the idea of a standard kitchen apron and designed an ingenious, functional artist's apron. This apron contains pockets for various working items such as scissors, paintbrushes, pens and pencils, a seam ripper, or any other item you use regularly. Wearing it can save you from wasting your precious studio time looking for the items you need close at hand. It's super-convenient for teachers who like to have instant access to chalk, markers and hand sanitizer. It's also a great idea for working artists who spend time at artist or craft shows. This apron would make a wonderful gift, and the fabric combinations are endless! Use pieces from your scrap pile to mix and match with your swap fabrics.

materials

fabric from swap

fabric in coordinating colors

sewing thread

twill tape

Note: To complete the project, the swap fabrics should total at least 1 yard (1m).

tools

iron and ironing board

rotary cutter and mat

scissors

sewing machine

straight pins

transparent ruler

Note: Use a ½" (1.5cm) seam allowance unless otherwise noted.

1 To make the apron as shown, cut front and back pieces measuring 11" × 25½" (28cm × 65cm). Cut 2 twill tape ties to fit the wearer.

2 To make the pocket piece, cut 9 strips of swap and coordinating fabrics measuring 8½" (21.5cm) long and 2"–4" (5cm–10cm) wide.

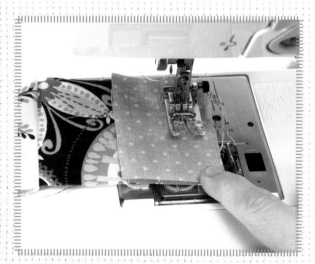

3 Cut 20 2½" (6.5cm) squares of different swap and coordinating fabrics. Sew the squares together to create a strip about 8½" (21.5cm) long. Repeat this step 2 more times to make 3 patchwork strips. Trim the strips to make them exactly 8½" (21.5cm) long.

4 Sew the strips together, alternating solid and patchwork strips randomly. Use a rotary cutter, mat and transparent ruler to evenly trim all the sides. Press the seams.

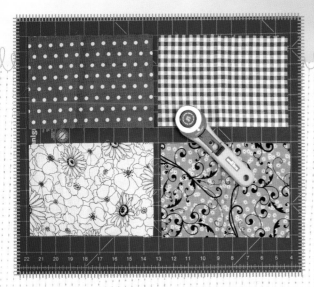

5 Cut 4 6" × 8½" (15cm × 21.5cm) blocks of swap fabric to line the back of the pocket. Sew the blocks together. Trim the pocket lining to the same size as the pocket front.

6 With right sides together, sew the pocket lining to the pocket front. Leave a 2" (5cm) opening at the bottom for turning. Clip the corners and turn the pocket right side out. Press, making sure to press the opening evenly. Your pocket should measure approximately 8" × 20" (20.5cm × 51cm).

7 Quilt the pocket in the desired design. (I used lines because you can use the patchwork seams as guides.)

8 Pin the pocket to the right side of the front apron piece; attach it to the fabric with a ¼" (6mm) seam on 3 sides, leaving the top open. Pin the pocket at 1½" (4cm), 4½" (11.5cm) and 11" (28cm) from the left side and sew down the pocket at the pins to divide the pocket into 4 sections.

9 Fold the end of each twill tape tie twice to hide the unfinished edge. Sew the fold down, securing it adequately; I used 2 rows of stitching. Pin each unfinished edge of the tie on the left and right front side of the apron, ¾" (2cm) from the top. The unfinished edge of the tie should line up with the unfinished edge of the fabric. Baste the ties in place and remove the pins.

10 Place the loose ends of the ties on top of the apron front. Place the apron back over the apron front, right sides together. Be aware of the ties in order to avoid sewing them where they do not belong. Sew around the apron, leaving a 2½" (6.5cm) opening for turning. Clip the corners.

11 Turn the apron right side out and press. Sew around the apron with a ¼" (6mm) seam to finish and close the opening.

Chapter 2

FABRIC JEWELRY AND ADORNMENTS

As a busy mom with four little ones, I have to admit that my clothing choices are often restricted to jeans and solid T-shirts. My biggest desire is just to remain clean! My favorite way to stay fashionable and keep to a budget is to accessorize with cute jewelry and hair pieces. While there is a large selection of jewelry available at decent prices in retail stores, I much prefer to make my own or support talented sewers who create their own jewelry. This chapter focuses on wonderful handmade pieces that will easily brighten up your wardrobe or make great gifts for others.

When we think of jewelry or other accessories, we often think of jewels, beads and metals. I love the juxtaposition of these three hard elements with the softness and variety of fabrics and papers. When you add the uniqueness of original artwork, you have a recipe for a one-of-a-kind wearable piece.

When creating wearable art pieces, keep your eye out for original mixed-media elements you can use. Antique stores can be great places to score good deals on vintage buttons and brooches. Save your leftover fabric scraps—even the tiny ones. When craft stores have sales, get a good deal on earring backs, pins, beading and fasteners. You can buy bead storage containers very inexpensively to store all your jewelry finds.

For this swap, we had five participating artists. Each artist made the same item five times, keeping one for herself and sending the other four items to each participant. In the end, each artist had five new handmade pieces. This swap is also a great way to exchange handmade ornaments, sewn artist trading cards (ATCs) or finished quilt squares. Keeping these types of swaps under ten people ensures that high-quality items will be exchanged.

ME AND MY PENGUIN

Designed by Danita Art

Danita Art's original style is highlighted in this fun brooch featuring a little girl and her penguin friend. Her design highlights the technique of transferring an original piece of artwork onto polymer clay. Polymer clay is a great resource when creating jewelry. It's flexible before it is baked, but when cooked it becomes hard and permanent.

You can vary this project greatly just by changing the image you use for transfer. Other variations when creating brooches include changing the size or shape of the transfer. You could add beads, fringe, or lace to the final piece. Also, you could vary the main image by printing it on fabric and then using embroidery thread or beading to highlight the art.

materials

clear polymer clay fixative

E-6000 glue

muslin

personal or copyright-free image

pin back

sewing thread

strongly brewed coffee

text from a vintage book

typing paper

white glue

white polymer clay

tools

clay roller

color laser printer

iron and ironing board

paintbrush

round cutter with 3" (7.5cm) diameter

scissors

sewing machine

spray bottle with water

 ## Creating Art in a Circular Shape

You have many choices when selecting a piece of art for your brooch. It could be a painting, a fabric piece, a photo or a copyright-free piece of art. To create a circular piece of art, scan the original into your computer. Using digital manipulation software (such as Adobe Photoshop), manipulate your image until you are happy with it. Create a circular boundary around the art. Set your printer so that the circle shape prints out approximately 3" (7.5cm) in diameter.

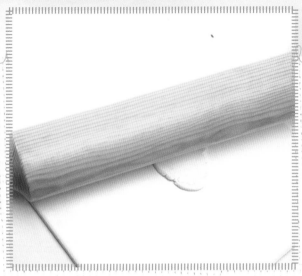

1 Print a design for your brooch onto typing paper with a color laser printer. (See Creating Art in a Circular Shape on page 51.) Make sure to print the image in reverse so the transfer will be facing the right way.

2 Condition a marble-sized amount of white polymer clay by kneading it and rolling it out.

3 Using a round cutter with a 3" (7.5cm) diameter, cut a circle of polymer clay.

4 Lay the circular piece of art face down on the polymer clay and spray it with water. Let it stand for a minute. When it is fully saturated, gently rub the paper with your finger until you remove all the paper fibers. Do this slowly and carefully so you don't rub the image off.

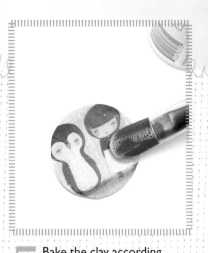

5 Bake the clay according to the manufacturer's instructions. Let it cool. Paint clear fixative over the image to protect it from smearing.

6 Stain a piece of muslin slightly larger than the clay piece by soaking it in strongly brewed coffee. Remove the fabric and rinse. After it dries, press the fabric to heat set the stain and remove wrinkles.

✿ TIP

The longer you soak the muslin in coffee, the darker it will be. If you don't want an even stain, fold the muslin and wrap it with rubber bands before submerging.

7 Cut 2 muslin circles slightly larger than the clay circle, varying their diameters by ¼" (6mm). Adhere a circle of text from a vintage book to each muslin circle using white glue. Place the smaller circle over the larger circle. Stitch them together with a straight stitch.

8 Using E-6000 glue, adhere the clay piece to the muslin circles. Attach a pin to the back.

FLOWER BUD EARRINGS

Designed by Jessica Fediw

Jessica Fediw's sewing style is so simple and clean, it's like a breath of fresh air. These earrings take almost no time and are fun to make. I plan to make a variety of these for myself and as gifts for others. Use different scraps of fabrics to create different looks. I think a pair made with muslin or burlap would be cute for someone who likes an earthy look. Tulle or sheer fabric would be great for someone with a very feminine style. Of course, different colors of fabrics could be catered to anyone's style. If you love this project, think of expanding on the theme and making a necklace. Enlarge the measurements of the fabric, and instead of sewing a bead in the middle, sew a tiny button with a hook. Make fifteen to twenty of them, and then string them up!

materials

E-6000 glue

2 earring posts

paint stick

2 seed beads

sewing thread

white muslin

tools

iron and ironing board

pencil

rubber stamp

scissors

sewing needle

small coin

1 Hold a 2" × 5" (5cm × 12.5cm) piece of white muslin over a rubber stamp of your choice. Using a paint stick, rub over the surface of the stamp until the image is visible.

2 Heat set the image with an iron.

3 Using a small coin as a template, trace 12 circles onto the back of the fabric.

4 Cut out the circles.

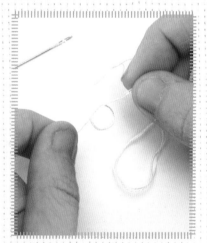

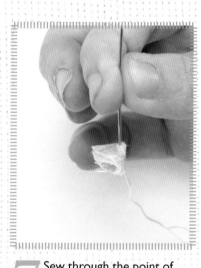

5 Thread a sewing needle with a piece of thread measuring 18" (45.5cm) long. Bring the ends of the thread together and tie a knot. When tying the knot, leave a loop in the thread to help secure the earring.

6 Make a petal by folding a circle in half. Fold it in half again.

7 Sew through the point of the first petal.

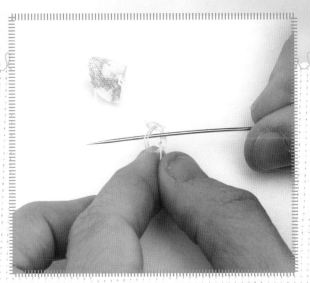

8   Pull the needle through the loop in the thread.

9   Fold and sew through the points of 5 more petals. Spread the petals into a circular shape.

10   Thread the needle through a seed bead and then sew back down through all the layers of fabric. Knot the thread to secure.

11   Using E-6000 glue, adhere an earring post to the back of the flower. Repeat Steps 5–11 to make another earring.

SOMEONE TO LOVE

Designed by Jenn McGlon

I started reading Jenn McGlon's blog a couple of years ago and have my own collection of her fun and whimsical work. In addition to her fantastic paintings, she also makes funky sculptures and dabbles in some fiber art pieces as well. For this headband, Jenn uses a combination of fabric and lace scraps and a handmade polymer clay pendant. This headband could be worn by a woman or varied to accommodate a little girl's style. Using the polymer clay to sculpt the focal point of the headband allows room for so much variety. You could create a basic design, like the heart in the oval that she creates, or you could opt for a more intricate piece.

materials

acrylic paints

black headband

black wool felt

clear polymer clay fixative

E-6000 glue

gel medium

muslin

polymer clay

sewing thread

text from a vintage book

vintage lace

tools

paintbrush

paper towel

scissors

sewing machine

sewing needle

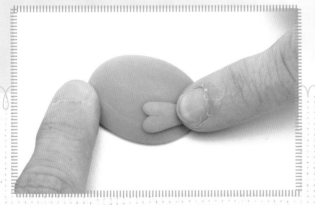

1 Form a small amount of polymer clay into an oval shape measuring approximately 2" (5cm) in length. Form a tiny heart with the polymer clay and add it to the top of the pendant by gently pressing. Follow the manufacturer's instructions for baking the clay. Let the pendant cool.

2 Paint the pendant with layers of acrylic paints. I used ecru, black and red paints. Apply a wash of brown paint and wipe away the excess with a paper towel for an antique look.

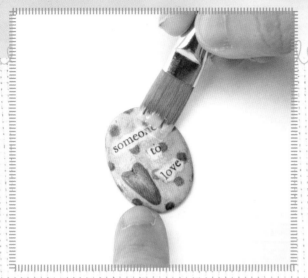

3 Cut out words from a vintage book and adhere them to the pendant using gel medium. Once dry, seal your pendant with a coat of clear polymer clay fixative.

4 Cut a piece of black wool felt a little larger than your pendant.

5 Using black thread, straight stitch several times down the length of a 3" × 7" (7.5cm × 18cm) piece of muslin.

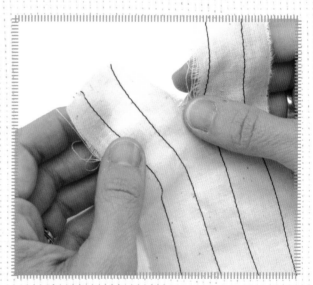

6 Tear the muslin in long strips, close to the sewn lines. Cut the strips into 3" (7.5cm) long pieces. Don't worry about cutting through the stitching; we are going for a deconstructed look.

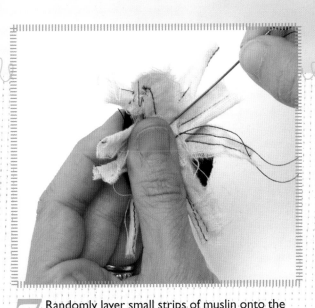

7 Randomly layer small strips of muslin onto the black wool piece. Sew through the center to secure all pieces of muslin to the wool.

8 Cut a 5" (12.5cm) piece of vintage lace. Using a needle and black thread, sew the muslin, wool and lace to the side of a headband, layering the lace first, then the wool and muslin strips.

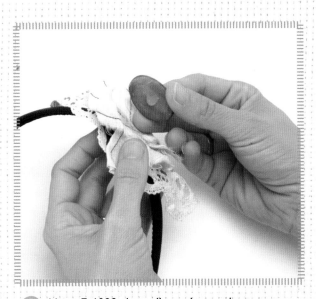

9 Using E-6000 glue, adhere the pendant over the center of the muslin strips. Let it dry and it's ready to wear!

CURIOUS CUFF

Designed by Alisa Burke

Alisa Burke's work is instantly recognizable. She uses bold, quick, painterly strokes and unpredictable free-form stitching. Her use of color is bright and brave. When you are following Alisa's technique, it is imperative that you "let go" of any rigid ideas you have about how you think things should look. This tutorial is a great exercise in having fun with your artwork. The cuff is created with layers of canvas that have been painted using different techniques. Experiment by painting random words or images on your canvas or fabric. Use pieces of a painting that you weren't happy with by tearing or cutting it up. Splatter paint, stamp your fabric or try techniques you've never tried before!

My favorite part of the cuff is the little book. What will be in yours? A poem or an inspirational quote? Perhaps you could fill it with your secret dreams or wishes . . . .

materials

acrylic paints

black elastic hair band

buttons

canvas

fabric scraps

scrap paper

sewing thread

twine

tools

paintbrush

rotary cutter and mat

scissors

sewing machine

sewing needle

straight pins

transparent ruler

Note: The measurements given for this project are based on an average woman's wrist.

1. Cut 2 pieces of canvas measuring 3" × 7¾" (7.5cm × 19.5cm) and paint them with acrylic paints as desired. These pieces are the front and back of the cuff. Let the paint dry. Set the back piece aside.

2. On the front piece, sew strips of colorful canvas or fabric scraps on top of each other using the decorative stitching of your choice.

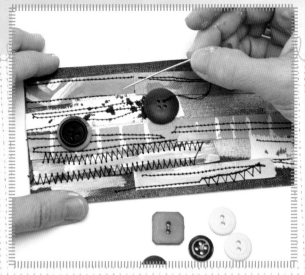

3 Once you are happy with your layers, hand sew buttons to the front piece. Leave a 1" (2.5cm) space on the left side and a 2" (5cm) space in the center. Have fun using different sizes, shapes and colors.

4 Cut a 1¾" × 3" (4.5cm × 7.5cm) piece of canvas for the cover of a tiny book.

5 Paint the top and bottom of the cover piece and sew across it with random lines of straight stitch.

6 Cut a small stack of scrap paper to measure 1½" × 2½" (4cm × 6.5cm) and fold it in half.

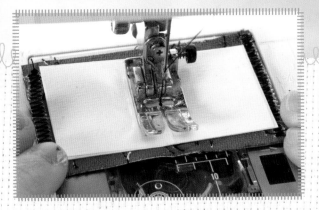

7 Place the folded stack of papers on top of the inside cover and sew along the fold using a straight stitch.

8 Hand sew a tiny button to the front cover. Machine sew a tiny loop made from twine onto the back cover for the closure.

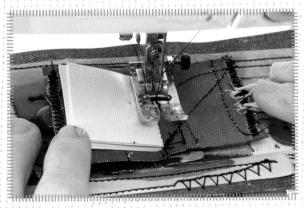

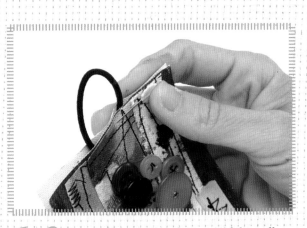

9 Sew the back flap of the book to the top piece of the cuff.

10 Lay the front and back pieces of the cuff together, wrong sides together. Pin an elastic hair band in between the 2 pieces.

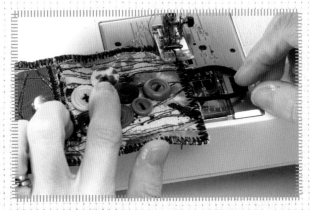

11 Zigzag stitch the 2 pieces together all the way around, securing the hair band. Remove the pin. It's ready to wear!

LOVE YOUR LIFE NECKLACE

Designed by Ruth Rae

In this project, Ruth Rae has created an exquisite piece that functions as both jewelry and art. The final piece is eccentric and delicate at the same time. It is a perfect example of the fine juxtaposition between the softness of the fabric pieces and the hardness of the metal jewelry links. I love how she has used free-form machine stitching to create different words for each part of the necklace.

This project could be varied in so many ways. Change the words to create a different message, or alter the entire color scheme in terms of fabrics and threads to create a whole new feel. You could make the circles into different shapes, or make the piece more complex by sewing many smaller circles and connecting them. Another slight variation would be to connect the fabric pieces with wire instead of embroidery thread. Some of your shapes could even contain images or a photograph.

materials

beads
brewed tea
clear nail polish
craft felt
embroidery thread
fabric strips
head pins
ink pad
muslin
necklace fastener
sewing thread
10mm silver jump rings
15mm silver jump rings

tools

chain-nose pliers
flush cutters
freemotion foot attachment
leather punch or Japanese screw punch
round-nose pliers
rotary cutter and mat
rubber stamp with text background
scissors
sewing machine
sewing needle

 ### Tea-Staining Muslin

Add an antique touch to muslin by staining it with tea. Boil a pot of water and place two to three tea bags inside. Let them steep for about 10 minutes. Remove the tea bags. Submerge the muslin and soak it for about 15 minutes.

1 Follow the instructions on page 67 to tea-stain 2 squares of muslin measuring 8" × 8" (20.5cm × 20.5cm). Remove the fabric and rinse. Do not press with an iron to maintain the wrinkles. Let the fabric dry.

2 Using a stamp with a text background and an ink pad, stamp all over the muslin squares.

3 Sandwich an 8" (20.5cm) square of craft felt between the 2 pieces of muslin.

4 Using a freemotion stitch, sew 6 circles and words onto the fabric sandwich.

5 Cut out the circles and punch holes in the tops with the smallest setting on a leather punch or a Japanese screw punch.

✿ TIP

If you're not comfortable sewing the words freehand, lightly write them on the fabric in pencil, and then trace with your sewing machine.

6 Connect the circles using embroidery thread and a needle. Pull the thread through the holes and knot it a few times. Fray the ends of the thread with the end of your needle, and then apply a small drop of clear nail polish to the knot to secure it.

7 Assemble the necklace chain by linking 10mm and 15mm jump rings until the chain is the desired length (see Jewelry-Making Tips below). Attach beaded head pins to some of the 10mm jump rings and sew small strips of fabric onto the necklace chain as desired. Add a necklace fastener to the top of the necklace.

8 Attach the ends of the necklace chain to the top left and right fabric circles with 2 10mm jump rings.

9 Attach a beaded dangle to the bottom circle with a jump ring.

Jewelry-Making Tips

• Open and close jump rings with two pairs of chain-nose pliers. When opening a jump ring, do not pull it open to the left and right, as this will damage the jump ring. Pull one side toward you and the other away. Close jump rings in the same manner.

• To assemble the beaded head pins, slide a bead onto a head pin and make a loop at the top with round-nose pliers. Wrap the excess wire around the base of the loop twice and then cut the excess wire with flush cutters.

• The beaded dangle is made from several beaded head pins attached to the end of a chain of three 10mm jump rings.

Chapter 3

ROUND ROBIN JOURNAL

There is something mysterious, exciting and satisfying about participating in a round robin collaboration. The book arrives to you in a box that has traveled to many far-away places. It has been in the hands of many other artists. You get to see what has been created so far, and you are inspired by the time and energy spent. You look forward to sending it to the next person to share your stitches.

When you participate in a round robin journal project—in this case, a fabric one—you will receive the book in the mail with instructions. You will normally have a firm time limit set to finish your piece. Remember to be aware of your time limit, and make sure to get it in the mail to the next participant on time. Remain true to your style and always sign your piece, but also carefully follow any instructions so the book has a cohesive format.

There are many different ways to create the "skeleton" of a round robin book. You can vary the size to make it smaller, or you can create a larger piece. If you decide to make the book large, make sure to mention shipping costs so the participants aren't shocked when mailing the project out. When I created the round robin book for this chapter, I wanted it to be accordion style so you could actually stand it up and open it all the way. I used cereal boxes as the page bases to give the participants a flat, sturdy surface to create on, but your book could be made from fabric as well. Be creative, but also consider the logistics.

For this project, I gave the participants a theme. I have my own collection of art entitled "She Said," where women are represented in an artistic manner and have something prolific to say. I wanted to see how everyone else would interpret this theme, and I was blown away by the final product's beauty and detail. The completed book was beyond my wildest expectations.

ASSEMBLING THE JOURNAL

materials

batting or interfacing
cereal boxes
fabric glue
muslin
sewing thread

tools

rotary cutter and mat
straight pins
scissors
sewing machine

template: page base
(see page 133)

transparent ruler

1 Flatten several cereal boxes and cut each box open so it is 1 large piece of cardboard. Use the provided template on page 133 to trace 2 page bases onto each piece of cardboard.

2 Cut out the page bases. Cut twice as many page bases as there are participants.

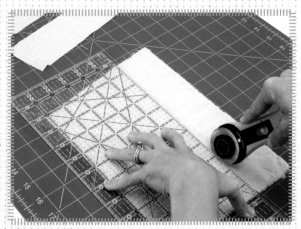

3 Cut strips of muslin measuring 2¼" × 9½" (5.5cm × 24cm) and strips of batting or interfacing measuring 2" × 9" (5cm × 23cm). Cut muslin strips equal to the number of page bases; cut half as many strips of batting or interfacing.

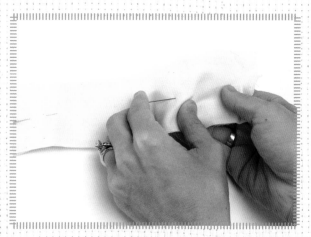

4 Make a sandwich with 2 muslin strips and a strip of batting or interfacing in the middle. Pin each sandwich together.

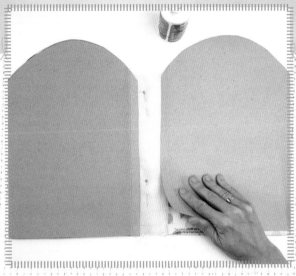

5 Using fabric glue, lightly adhere a binding strip ¼" (6mm) in from the edge of 1 of the page bases to secure it for sewing. Apply glue to the top of the binding strip and adhere a second page base on top of the first page base.

6 Repeat Step 5 on the unglued side of the binding strip.

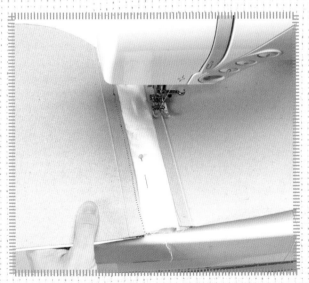

7 Sew 2 lines of straight stitch down the page base sandwich where the binding strip is glued. Do this for both page base sandwiches.

8 Repeat this process until all the page bases are connected. The book will fold back and forth like an accordian.

she said,
"today I will celebrate my
favorite things..."

dream

MY FAVORITE THINGS

Designed by Jenn McGlon

In Jenn McGlon's round robin page, she wanted to highlight a few of her favorite things. By scanning original art work or using copyright-free images, you can print directly on fabric using a standard ink-jet printer. Craft and hobby stores do sell fabric paper that is ready to be fed into your printer, but it can get very costly. Jenn demonstrates how to use freezer paper and muslin to get the same effect at a much lower price! I love this technique because you can expand on it in many ways. Use a white or cream-colored muslin, or experiment with printing on other colors or lightweight materials. Print out an image in black and white on fabric and then embellish it with fabric paints and embroidery. You can also use this technique to print images for quilts and home décor items.

materials

acrylic paints

buttons

cardboard page base (see page 72)

fabric scraps

fiberfill

freezer paper

matte gel medium

muslin

personal or copyright-free images or paintings

sewing thread

vintage book pages

vintage earrings, charms, lockets, lace or ribbons

tools

ink-jet printer

iron and ironing board

round paint pouncer

scissors

sewing machine

sewing needle

small and medium paintbrushes

1 Use the freezer paper method (see page 12) to create fabric that can be printed on. Print your own paintings or copyright-free images onto the fabric. Cut the printed images out, leaving small borders for sewing. Remove the freezer paper and fray the edges of each image with your fingers for a shabby look.

2 Attach squares of vintage book pages to the page base (excluding the top arch) using matte gel medium. Once dry, add acrylic paints to create a textured look. Use earthy tones, with splashes of blues, pinks and reds. Use a pouncer to make polka dots in turquoise.

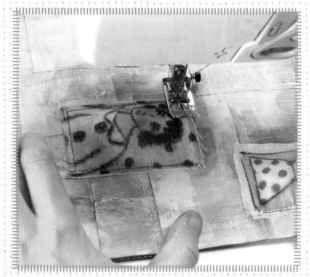

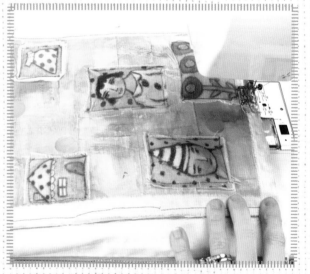

3 Sew the printed images to the page using red thread with a straight stitch. Sew 3 sides of each image, stuff with a little bit of fiberfill, and then sew the fourth side shut.

4 Tear strips of muslin and sew them onto each side of the page and the bottom to make borders. Try to achieve a primitive, shabby look by using a fast and crazy stitch—no perfect lines!

5 Cut out, tear and fray the edges of a piece of muslin to cover the arch shape of the page base. Sew the muslin in place with a straight stitch, leaving a small opening. Stuff the top arch with fiberfill and then sew the opening closed.

6 Embellish the page by hand sewing vintage buttons, bits of old lace and muslin. Some other choices include vintage earrings, charms, lockets or pieces of ribbon.

7 Hand paint a few more of your favorite things on the page with acrylic paint. I painted 2 little boys (for my sons) and a little red bird flying by.

8 Tear words out of a vintage book for your quote, or type and print them out. My quote says, "She said 'Today I will celebrate my favorite things.'" Attach the words to the muslin using gel medium.

"Don't Worry" She ★ said

everything will be OK

EVERYTHING WILL BE O.K.

Designed by Catherine Thursby

Catherine Thursby's technique for her round robin page focuses on fabric painting. She simply uses her fabric as she would a canvas or paper by painting directly on it with acrylics. There are many things to consider when painting on fabric. Tightly woven cotton fabrics are the easiest to work with, but you can paint on rayons and silks as well. I suggest doing a small sample before working on your final fabric to play with the results. Iron your fabric before beginning, as wrinkles will easily offset your design. If you are painting on fabrics that will be washed, make sure to use fabric paints and heat set the dry paint with an iron. You can use your paints to stamp and stencil on fabric, too. Make sure you have wax paper or an old towel underneath your fabric because it will most likely bleed through. If you really enjoy fabric painting, you may consider purchasing fabric markers. These allow a little more control and make it much easier to create small details and thin lines.

materials

acrylic paints

basting spray

batting

black fine point permanent marker

black, olive green and white craft felt

blue cotton fabric

cardboard page base (see page 72)

freezer paper

linen

muslin

sewing thread

tools

iron and ironing board

pencil

pinking shears

scissors

sewing machine

small and medium paintbrushes

small bowl

wax paper

1 Cut a piece of linen a little larger than the page base.

2 Using a small bowl as a guide, trace a circle on a piece of blue cotton with a pencil. Lay it on a piece of wax paper. Draw in some shapes to resemble continents on the earth. Using green and brown acrylic paint, fill in the shapes. Set it aside to dry.

3 Draw and cut out a large bird from white felt. Using cream, white, and gray acrylic paints, shade the bird. Paint its eye, cheek and beak. Cut a piece of batting to fit underneath.

4 Iron a piece of muslin onto freezer paper using the freezer paper method (see page 12). Paint it cream and let it dry. Write the phrases *Don't worry* and *she said* on the muslin. Use a fine point brush to paint the letters black and let them dry. Cut the muslin with pinking shears and set it aside. Cut out a smaller piece of muslin and use a black fine point permanent marker to write the phrase *everything will be*.

5 Draw a woman with her arms outstretched on a piece of muslin. Iron the muslin onto freezer paper using the freezer paper method. Paint the drawing with various colors of acrylic paint. Outline the woman with a black fine point permanent marker. Cut the drawing out, leaving a small border around the figure for stitching.

6 Cut out the letters *O* and *K* from black felt. Draw and cut out a long leaf from olive green felt.

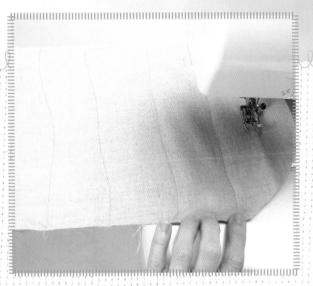

7 Using beige thread and a straight stitch, sew across the linen in random lines to attach the piece to the page base.

8 Spray the linen with a light coat of basting spray. (Do this in a place with adequate ventilation.) Lay the earth piece on the linen. Use blue thread and a satin stitch to outline the earth.

9 Lay the remaining pieces on the linen. Use yellow thread and a straight stitch to sew on the woman. Use black thread and a straight stitch for the lettering. Use gray thread and a straight stitch to sew on the bird and leaf.

SHE SAID.... I'D RATHER ASK FORGIVENESS THAN PERMISSION.

ASKING FORGIVENESS

Designed by Kristen Feighery

I am very fond of Kristen Feighery's folk art style and her renderings of biblical stories. Her interpretation of the classic Eve story gets a new twist in her round robin page. While the first thing you may notice is her painting technique of acrylics on top of the black gesso, her sewing technique focuses on hand embroidery. Embroidery has a long history as a creative pleasure among women for generations. In the last few years embroidery has made a popular comeback. Sewers are pursuing the various possibilities that thread possesses in fiber art projects. Aside from just a needle and thread, other materials, such as beads, sequins, semiprecious stones and metal strips can be used as part of this decorative stitching technique. Although hand embroidery can be time-consuming, it is a great way to slow down and can even be relaxing.

materials

acrylic paints
assorted ribbons
assorted scrapbooking papers
black gesso
cardboard page base (see page 72)
fabric glue
fabric scraps
fiberfill
gloss gel medium
sewing thread
sticky-back canvas
white colored pencil

tools

alphabet rubber stamps
insect rubber stamp
scissors
sewing machine
sewing needle
small and medium paintbrushes
small coin

1 Cut a piece of sticky-back canvas to fit the page base, but do not adhere it yet. Paint the canvas with black gesso and let it dry.

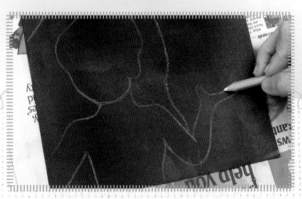

2 Draw the images of a woman, snake and tree with a white colored pencil.

3 Begin painting the images with acrylic paints. Start with the whites of the eyes, and then paint the lips, face and hair. Leave a very thin line of black gesso showing between each element. Paint the background last.

4 Using a small coin as a template, trace 20 circles onto the backs of assorted scrapbooking papers. Cut 2 leaf shapes from the papers. Decoupage the circles onto the tree and the leaves onto Eve's chest using gloss gel medium.

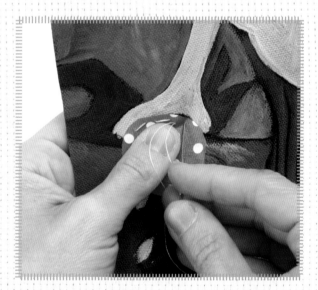

5 Cut 1 large circle and 6 small circles from fabric scraps. Hand sew 4 of the small circles onto the tree. Sew the large circle into the palm of Eve's hand and the remaining 2 small circles onto her chest. For all the circles, leave a small opening for stuffing. Stuff the circles with fiberfill and sew the openings shut.

6 Using alphabet rubber stamps and white acrylic paint, stamp a quote above Eve's head. Stamp an insect in white paint in the lower right corner.

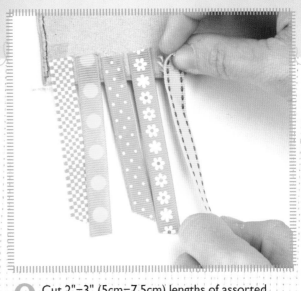

7 Seal the page with gloss gel medium, carefully avoiding the fabric elements.

8 Cut 2"–3" (5cm–7.5cm) lengths of assorted ribbon and glue them along the bottom edge of the page base with fabric glue.

9 Adhere the painting to the page base. Cut 2 pieces of ribbon measuring 9½" (24cm) for the side borders and 1 piece measuring 8" (20.5cm) for the bottom edge. Cut 4 pieces measuring 3" (7.5cm) and curve them around the top arch of the page. Glue the ribbon borders in place. Straight stitch over the ribbon. Straight stitch around the tree in random lines to add texture.

SHE FOLLOWS HER HEART

Designed by Alisa Burke

Adding three-dimensional items to fabric art is one way to add a new dynamic to your projects. Alisa Burke's technique on her round robin page focuses on creating a 3-D object out of canvas pieces and fabric. True to her style, Alisa's page features torn strips and bold, colorful strokes. Creating a 3-D object is as simple as stuffing a cut-out shape with fiberfill and sewing it shut. To create more depth, consider embroidering your shape with beads or embroidery thread before stuffing it. The resulting texture will definitely be the focal point. One thing I love about fabric art is the tactile sensation you experience while sewing. This project is a great way to highlight that experience.

materials

acrylic paints

assorted scrapbooking papers, newspapers, old maps and pages from books

black fine tip permanent marker

canvas

cardboard page base (see page 72)

fabric glue

fabric paints

fiberfill

2 old paintbrushes

sewing thread

white colored pencil

yarn or fiber scraps

tools

freemotion foot attachment

paintbrushes

pencil

scissors

sewing machine

sewing needle

template: page base (see page 133)

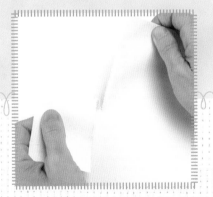

1 Tear pieces of canvas into different sizes to cover the page base.

2 Using different techniques such as colorwashing, splattering and layering, paint the pieces with your desired colors of acrylic and fabric paints. Feel free to mix in other papers such as old maps, pages out of books or scrapbooking paper.

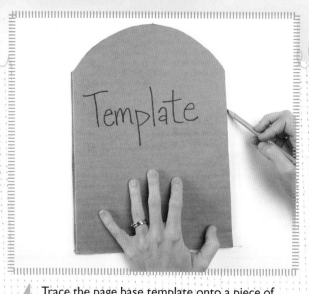

3 Cut a piece of canvas in the shape of a heart. Using the techniques from Step 2, paint an abstract design on the heart. Let the paint dry. Using a black fine tip permanent marker, write the quote on the heart: "She said she would always follow her heart."

4 Trace the page base template onto a piece of canvas and cut it out.

5 Using fabric glue, lightly adhere all the painted pieces of canvas onto the page base canvas.

6 Change the walking foot on your sewing machine to the freemotion foot. Sew the pieces of painted canvas using a random stitch.

7 Sew fiber or yarn scraps in random spots on the painted canvas.

8 Write the same quote from Step 3 onto the painted canvas using a white colored pencil.

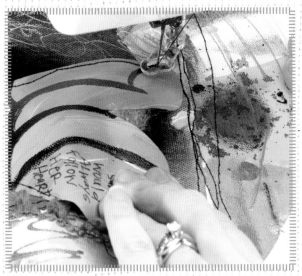

9 Sew the heart to the canvas, leaving an opening large enough to stuff the heart with fiberfill. Stuff the heart, and then sew the heart closed.

10 Hand sew old paintbrushes to the canvas, sewing in several places to secure. Attach the canvas page to the cardboard page base with a straight stitch.

SECRETS

Designed by Claudine Hellmuth

Claudine Hellmuth combines her unique style with recycled materials to create her round robin piece. By using a stained shirt that had belonged to her husband and some old bottle caps, she gives new meaning to incorporating "green" elements into a mixed-media piece. There are many ways to recycle when making fabric creations. Follow Claudine's lead and embellish your projects with used or found objects. These could be items around the house, or items that you have found in nature. Or, you can join the "Use What You Have" revolution and refrain from buying any new fabric or supplies for thirty days. Use only what you have in your stash or find ways to recycle items in your house. Save all of your fabric scraps, even the teeny tiny ones, to use in miniature art quilts or artist trading cards.

materials

acrylic paints

black and white photo or copyright-free image

black fine point permanent marker

cardboard page base (see page 72)

fabric scraps

ink pad

matte gel medium

old shirt

2 recycled bottle caps

sewing thread

sticky-back canvas

tools

hot glue gun and glue sticks

ink-jet printer

leaf rubber stamp

paintbrush

sewing machine

1 Enlarge and print a black and white photo or a copyright-free image onto sticky-back canvas and cut it out. Use acrylic paints to enhance the photo. In this instance, I painted the dress a bright orange and outlined it with a black fine point permanent marker.

2 Cut a large piece of blue fabric to cover about half the page base. (I used a shirt that my husband spilled ink on and could no longer wear.) Glue the fabric to the page base using matte gel medium.

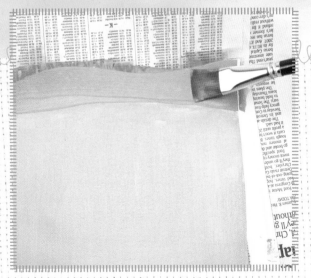

3 Paint green hills in 2 different shades onto sticky-back canvas and cut them out. Adhere them under the blue fabric sky.

4 Paint 2 white clouds onto sticky-back canvas and cut them out. Outline them with a black fine point permanent marker.

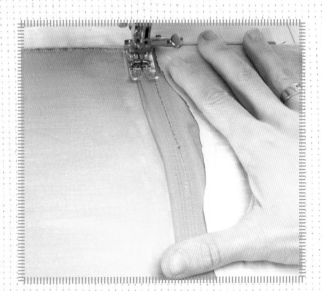

5 Outline the hills with orange, red and yellow threads and a straight stitch.

6 Adhere the girl to the right side of the page. Adhere the clouds in the sky.

7 Draw 3 flower outlines with a black fine point permanent marker.

8 Stamp a leaf print onto a 1" × 5" (2.5cm × 12.5cm) strip of sticky-back canvas. Adhere this strip at the bottom of the page, below the flowers. Extend the flower stems onto this strip.

9 Clean 2 used bottle caps and let them dry. Cut 2 circles of fabric to fit inside the caps and adhere them with gel medium. Using hot glue, adhere the bottle caps to the insides of the flower outlines.

CONTRIBUTING ARTISTS

ALL YOU NEED IS LOVE
Danita Art

BRAVER THAN SHE THOUGHT
Sarah Wyman

CUPCAKES
Chrissie Grace

FEELINGS ARE EVERYWHERE
Sandy Mastroni

she said, we all need

grace
to grow

GRACE TO GROW
Ruth Rae

she said

her heart

blossomed

in the

garden

HER HEART BLOSSOMED
IN THE GARDEN
Heather Sleightholm

LIVE, LAUGH, LOVE
Lori Vliegen

MORE COLOR
Sara Mincy

Chapter 4

COLLABORATIVE ART QUILT

There are many different ways to collaborate with others on a sewing theme. Art quilts are a popular project right now, so I decided it would be fun to create an art quilt triptych. I did not designate a theme, although every participant had to make their quilt block the same size: 10½" × 10½" (26.5cm × 26.5cm). I decided on this size because I wanted the finished product to be very large. For the sake of variety, I also assigned everyone a different technique to showcase. For example, Yetta Miller worked with Lutrador, Catherine Thursby incorporated wire into hers, and Kristen Feighery worked with transparencies. These types of assignments are not necessary, but they sometimes help people break out of their proverbial boxes.

The quilt blocks were formed by making a fabric sandwich with a bottom piece of fabric, a middle piece of batting and a top piece, which was altered in various ways. When the top piece was complete, the sandwich was fused together usually by sewing all three layers together. Using a grommet punch and ⅜" (1cm) grommets, I inserted holes at the top and bottom of each quilt block for connecting. I chose natural rope to hang them together, but you could use ribbon or even strands of beading instead.

I wanted the final piece of collaborative art to hang, which is why I chose the triptych style. Other variations could include making a soft book by binding all of the blocks together, or assembling them to form a traditional quilt. The quilt blocks could be made in varying sizes, including a tiny 2½" × 3½" (6.5cm × 9cm), which is the size of an artist trading card. Artist trading cards (or ATCs) are very popular original pieces of art that are created with the intention of swapping, not selling. You could organize a gigantic collaboration of ATC quilt blocks, which I'm sure would make a fascinating wall hanging.

MYSTERIOUS MAJESTY

Designed by Ruth Rae

There is no other word to describe Ruth Rae's work but exceptional. Her sewing projects are filled with depth, originality, layers of poetry and meticulous free-form images. Aside from fabric, she uses a large variety of materials such as paper, resin, photography and natural findings. You can take all the techniques Ruth presents and get lost in a world of eclectic visions.

For this project, pick a theme that really means something to you. You could start with an old photograph that has sentimental value. Find lace or embroidered pieces that reflect a vintage style. Pick a color palette that suits your fancy. Create or use stamps that will subtly reflect the message you want to convey. While you may be learning new techniques, focus on the poetry of the piece. Remember to make it your own.

materials

beige, brown and burgundy craft felt

black lace

brewed tea

burgundy ink pad

button

embroidery thread

fabric paper

fiberfill

freezer paper
(optional; for freezer paper method)

image of a face

muslin

page from a vintage book

tulle

two-part epoxy resin

small twig

tools

foam brush

freemotion foot attachment

garbage bag

heat gun

ink-jet printer

rotary cutter and mat

rubber stamp with text

scissors

sewing machine

sewing needle

transparent ruler

1 Cut a 10½" (26.5cm) square of tea-stained muslin (see page 67). Use a burgundy ink pad and a text stamp to stamp all over the muslin.

2 Use a heat gun to carefully burn holes into a 10" (25.5cm) square of brown felt and an 8" × 10" (20.5cm × 25.5cm) piece of burgundy felt to create an aged look.

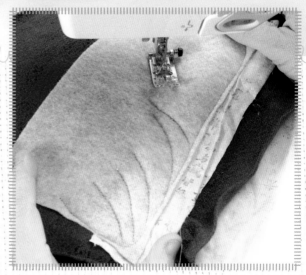

3 Layer the brown felt and burgundy felt on top of the muslin. With embroidery thread, blanket stitch around the burgundy felt, sewing through all the layers. Blanket stitch the brown felt to the muslin.

4 Cut 2 strips of muslin measuring 1½" × 5" (4cm × 12.5cm) and 1½" × 7" (4cm × 18cm). Cut a 4" × 7" (10cm × 18cm) piece of beige felt. Use a freemotion stitch to attach the strips to the burgundy felt.

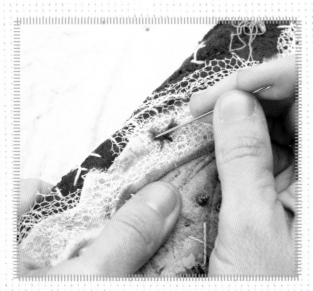

5 Attach a 3" × 9" (7.5cm × 23cm) strip of tulle with small pieces of embroidery thread tied into knots. Fray the ends of the embroidery thread with a needle.

6 Cover your work surface with a plastic garbage bag. Mix two-part epoxy resin following the manufacturer's instructions. Apply the resin to a page from a vintage book with a foam brush. Let it cure overnight. Attach the book page to the quilt block using white embroidery thread and cross stitches.

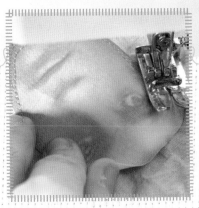

7 Cut a 5" × 6" (12.5cm × 15cm) piece of muslin. Print out an image of a face onto fabric paper, or use the freezer paper method (see page 12). Cut it out and sew it to the muslin with a freemotion stitch, leaving a small opening to stuff with fiberfill. Sew the opening closed.

8 Cut a piece of black lace in the shape of a crown and sew it above the head with french knots and cross stitches.

9 Sew the muslin with the face to the quilt block. Add french knots to this muslin and the beige felt with light brown embroidery thread.

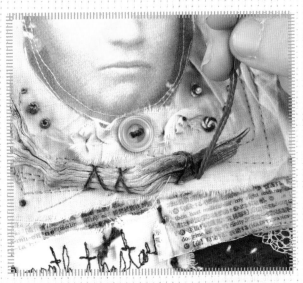

10 Fold a piece of muslin in half. Using freemotion stitching, sew the phrases *let's take a walk* and *beneath the stars* onto the muslin. Cut out the strips of wording. Sew these strips above and below the face with small pieces of brown embroidery thread tied into knots. Fray the embroidery thread with a needle.

11 Hand sew a button and a small twig below the face.

TREE LOVER

Designed by Danita Art

Whether you are looking at Danita Art's paintings, sculptures, dolls or fiber art, there is no mistaking her distinct style. Her art is a combination of complex layers and a simple and refreshing human figure. For Danita's quilt block, I asked her to use a natural dye to dye some fabric used in the quilt. In the past, all fabrics were dyed naturally, and there are still many advantages to using natural dyes. Natural dyes produce less harmful waste than their chemical counterparts, and are more environmentally friendly. Danita dyed her fabric with turmeric, which can be easily found in the spice section of your local grocer. Many materials can be used for dyeing fabrics, including different roots, nuts and flowers as well as common fruits and vegetables. You'll be surprised at the vast array of colors you can create. The lighter the fabric color, the better saturation you will achieve. Try working with muslin, silk, cotton and wool for the best results.

materials

- batting
- fabric paper (optional)
- fabric scraps
- freezer paper
- fusible web
- ground tumeric
- muslin
- personal or copyright-free image of a girl
- sewing thread

tools

- freemotion foot attachment
- ink-jet printer
- iron and ironing board
- rotary cutter and mat
- scissors
- sewing machine
- stainless steel saucepan
- straight pins
- tablespoon
- transparent ruler
- water (for soaking and dyeing fabric)
- wooden spoon

1 Cut out 2 pieces of muslin measuring 10½" × 10½" (26.5cm × 26.5cm). Soak the fabric in tap water and wring it out. Set it aside.

2 To make the dye, stir 4 tablespoons of ground turmeric into 2 pints of water in a large stainless steel saucepan. Bring the mixture to a boil and let it simmer for about 15 minutes. Stir with a wooden spoon or plastic stirring utensil. Allow it to cool slightly.

3 Submerge the damp muslin in the hot dye. Soak it for as long as you like to allow the color to develop. Use a wooden spoon to stir the liquid and ensure that the fabric is evenly covered. Allow it to dry completely, and then iron out the wrinkles.

 TIP

If you would like a richer color, remove the fabric, wring and allow it to dry, then re-soak it in the dye. Repeat this process until you get the color you want. Once you are happy with the color of the fabric, rinse it under a faucet until the water runs clear.

4 Draw and paint an image of a girl, or use a copyright-free image. Scan it into your computer and print it onto muslin using the freezer paper method (see page 12), or use fabric paper. Iron the image onto fusible interfacing.

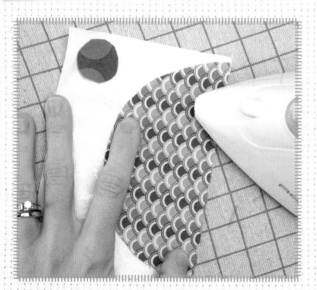

5 Cut a hill shape to fit the bottom of the quilt block from green print fabric. Cut a circle from another green print fabric for the tree. Iron both pieces onto fusible web.

6 Iron scraps of pink and yellow fabric onto fusible web and cut out a butterfly. Repeat this process to cut out a scarf.

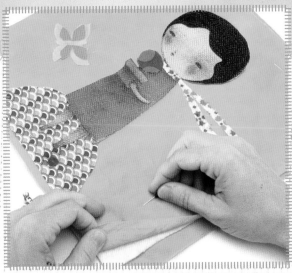

7 Arrange all the pieces onto a 10½" (26.5cm) piece of dyed muslin. Use an iron to fuse the pieces in place.

8 Layer the other 10½" (26.5cm) square of dyed muslin, a 10" (25.5cm) square of batting and the top piece of fabric to make a quilt sandwich. Pin the squares together.

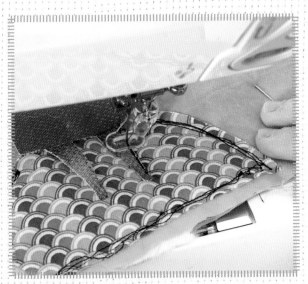

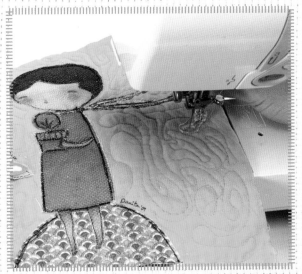

9 Change the walking foot to the freemotion foot on your sewing machine. Using black thread and a freemotion stitch, outline all the fabric elements.

10 Using a thread that matches the dyed fabric, run a freemotion stitch all over the quilt block to finish the quilt. Remove the pins.

RUSTED REMEMBRANCE

Designed by Heather Sleightholm

The first time I came across folk artist Heather Sleightholm's work, I was smitten. Her vintage style focuses on the pioneer spirit. In her own words, she is inspired by "the beauty of her prairie home, a good ghostly tale and details from a time long ago." The technique of rusting objects to age them fits her style perfectly. Rusted items appear to be aged and weathered and can add a lot of aesthetic appeal and vintage charm to your artwork. You can find rusting kits at craft stores; however, you can create your own rusty items at virtually no cost by following Heather's tutorial.

materials

batting

fabric for quilt top and backing

fabric glue

metallic acrylic paints

muslin

personal or copyright-free image

sewing thread

transfer paper

various fabrics to be rusted: ribbons, upholstery fabric, lace and crochet doilies

various metal objects to be rusted: antique buttons and a locket

tools

hot glue gun and glue sticks

ink-jet printer

iron and ironing board

large plastic bag

rotary cutter and mat

rusty can

scissors

sewing machine

sewing needle

straight pins

toothbrush

transparent ruler

vinegar

water (for rusting objects)

1 Cut out 2 10½" (26.5cm) squares of fabric for the quilt top and backing. Gather fabric bits such as ribbon, upholstery fabric, lace and crochet doilies. Gather a few metal objects as well, such as antique buttons and a locket.

2 Follow the instructions on page 110 to rust the gathered items.

Transferring Rust

In a bowl mix three parts vinegar with one part water and soak any cloth items you are planning to rust for a few minutes. (I recommend doing this step outside because of the strong smell of the vinegar.) After wringing out the excess liquid, place the cloth items, as well as any metal items, in a large plastic bag with a rusty can. Any rusty item will serve well for the transfer, and the rustier the better!

Drape the cloth items around the can; the metal items can sit in the bottom of the bag. Set the entire bag in the backyard in full sun. Keep the bag open to aid the oxidation. For a good dirty rust, leave the items in the bag with the rusted can for about 24 hours.

If you find that you want more rust on your cloth items, rewet them in the vinegar/water mixture and return them to the bag with the rusty can. Remember, the more direct contact the cloth has with the rusted object, the more rust it will absorb.

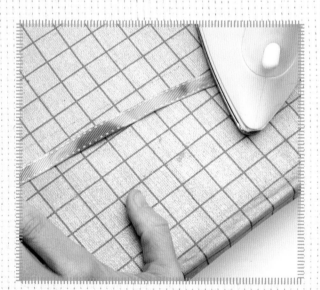

3 When the fabric is rusted to satisfaction, lay it flat to dry (preferably outside). Iron the wrinkles out of the fabric elements.

4 Print a personal painting or a copyright-free image onto transfer paper, following the manufacturer's instructions. Remember to print the image in reverse. Cut out the image and iron it onto a piece of plain muslin. Let the paper cool and then carefully peel off the transfer paper.

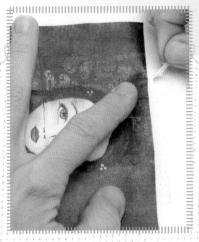

5 Snip the edges of the muslin and carefully rip with your fingers to create a ragged effect.

6 To create the illusion of rust on the painting, lightly splatter the image with metallic copper and bronze acrylic paint by flicking your thumb across a paint-soaked toothbrush.

7 Arrange the rusted fabrics, ribbon and the transferred painting on the quilt top fabric as desired. Once arrangement is decided, lightly adhere the pieces to the quilt top with fabric glue and then stitch them down.

8 Hand sew the rusted locket and a small piece of ribbon to the quilt block.

9 Layer the quilt backing, a 10" (25.5cm) piece of batting and the quilt top to make a sandwich. Pin the square together. Sew the fabric squares and batting together with a straight stitch. Use hot glue to adhere the rusted antique buttons.

TOGETHER

Designed by Sarah Wyman

Sarah Wyman's artwork is a delightful combination of collage and painting. The women she creates have very unique, ponderous eyes—I often wonder what they are thinking! In this piece, I love that the women are holding hands, symbolizing a relationship that runs parallel with the bond that is created by participating in swaps or collaborations. It is this together-ness that takes our unique and individual styles and stories and mixes them into a beautiful and cohesive final product. This piece also represents the friendships that form when collaborating with other artists. As artists and sewers, our souls are spilled into our work. It takes vulnerability and courage to share our work with other people, to be open to learning new things, and to be able to let go of the things that don't work. Remember this when you work with other people. Be open to constructive criticism. Be willing to take risks. Remember that you are involved because you wanted to evolve.

materials

acrylic paints

batting

drawing paper

embroidery thread

fabric for quilt backing

fabric glue

fiber art paper

flowers suitable for drying

fusible web

matte gel medium

muslin

pages from an old atlas

sewing thread

yarn

tools

iron and ironing board

microwave flower press (see page 12)

paintbrush

pencil

rotary cutter and mat

scissors

sewing machine

sewing needle

straight pins

transparent ruler

tweezers

1 Paint a 10½" (26.5cm) square of fiber art paper with a wash of blue. Paint a green strip across the bottom of the page.

2 Tear strips from an old atlas page and attach them to the art paper with matte gel medium. Coat the entire page with matte medium. Lightly paint a blue wash over the strips of atlas so you can still see them.

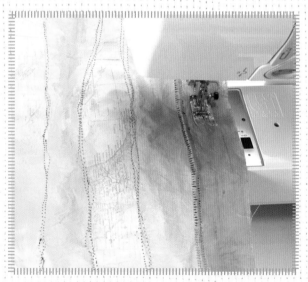

3 Iron a 10½" (26.5cm) square of fusible webbing adhesive to the back of the painted art paper. Peel off the backing, place a 10½" (26.5cm) square of muslin onto the fusible web and iron again. Never iron directly on the fiber art paper!

4 Using a straight stitch and black thread, outline the strips of atlas. Using a zigzag stitch and green thread, sew 3 rows on the painted green strip for grass.

5 To make the girls, draw faces on drawing paper or scraps of atlas paper. Paint the features and cut out their heads.

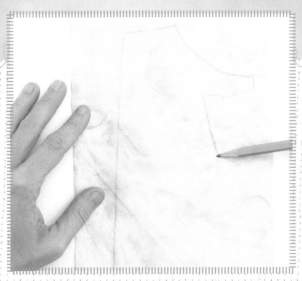

6 Draw dress shapes on different colors of fiber art paper, but don't cut them out. Iron a 10½" (26.5cm) square of fusible web to the back of the paper. Peel off the backing, place a 10½" (26.5cm) square of muslin onto the fusible web and iron again.

7 Using a microwave flower press (see page 12), dry some small flowers. Experiment with different kinds of flowers, as some of them change colors after they have been dried.

8 Using matte gel medium and a pair of tweezers, carefully glue the flowers onto each of the dress outlines. Cover both dresses with matte medium and let them dry. Using a straight stitch, outline the flowers.

9 Cut out the dresses. Lay out the heads and dresses and attach the heads to the background paper with a straight stitch. Attach the dresses using a straight stitch, then zigzag stitch around them. Sew freemotion lines for the hair.

10 Using embroidery thread, hand sew lines of running stitch in the sky, french knots inside the flowers and a running stitch around each dress.

11 Layer a 10½" (26.5cm) square of backing fabric, a 10" (25.5cm) square of batting and the quilt top to make a sandwich. Pin the squares together. Sew around the block with a straight stitch. Adhere yarn around the edges of the block with fabric glue and then secure with a zigzag stitch.

MOLOKAI
KALAWAO COUNTY
(Leper Settlement)

INSPIRATION GARDEN

Designed by Lori Vleigen

In this project, Lori Vleigen translates her beautiful and clean style into handmade stamps. For her quilt block, she created her own stamps to use on the fabric. If you would like to carve your own stamps, there are many tutorials online to lead you through the process. You will need carving blocks, carving handles and a pencil. However, you can also find a huge variety of stamps in any craft store. When stamping, keep a few things in mind. If you are stamping on fabric that will not be washed, you can use a large variety of materials, such as paint or regular stamp pads, to ink the stamp. Otherwise, you will need to use inks and paints that have been formulated to be heat set for permanency on fabric. Always practice on scrap fabrics before you commit to the real project, and always re-ink your stamp for each impression. Use smooth fabrics, as textured ones can alter your stamped images.

materials

batting

buttons

embroidery thread

fabric for quilt top, backing and rectangles

fabric glue

fabric paint

ink pad

muslin

seed beads

tools

alphabet rubber stamps

paintbrush

rotary cutter and mat

rubber or handmade stamps of flowers and leaves

scissors

sewing needle

straight pins

transparent ruler

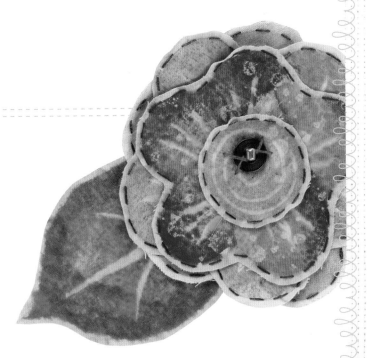

1 Cut a 10½" (26.5cm) square of fabric for the quilt top. Cut a 9½" (24cm) square of batting.

2 Cut a 10" (25.5cm) square of coordinating fabric for the top layer. Using a leaf stamp, stamp the entire surface with a very thin layer of fabric paint. Cut this fabric and the batting into rectangles measuring 2¾" × 3¾" (7cm × 9.5cm), 2¾" × 5¾" (7cm × 14.5cm), 4¾" × 6¾" (12cm × 17cm) and 5¾" × 6¾" (14.5cm × 17cm).

 TIP

Instead of dipping stamps directly into the paint, use a paintbrush to apply a thin, even layer onto the stamp.

3 Use flower stamps and fabric paint to stamp flowers onto small pieces of muslin. One flower stamp should be slightly larger than the other. Create 6 large flowers and 3 slightly smaller flowers. Create 3 flower centers by stamping spiral circles onto muslin. Cut out the shapes.

4 Stamp, stitch and cut leaves using the same method as in Step 3.

5 Sew around the edges of each flower using 2 strands of embroidery thread and a running stitch. Cut out the flower shapes. Use a stamp pad to distress the edges, if desired.

6 Assemble 3 flower layers by stacking a small flower and a flower center on top of 2 larger flowers using fabric glue. Glue a button to the center of each circle.

7 Assemble the quilt block by layering the leaf-stamped rectangles on top of the corresponding batting rectangles. Arrange them on the quilt top as shown on page 123 and secure with pins.

8 Hand sew a row of straight stitches in between each rectangle. Sew seed beads running parallel to the edges of the quilt top. Leave a 4" (10cm) gap at the bottom right for the stamped title.

9 Glue stamped leaves and assembled flowers onto the quilt top. Hand sew the flowers to the quilt, sewing through all the layers.

10 Using alphabet stamps and ink, stamp the title "Inspiration Garden" onto a piece of fabric. Trim around the edges and glue the piece onto the quilt top. Blanket stitch around the piece to secure it.

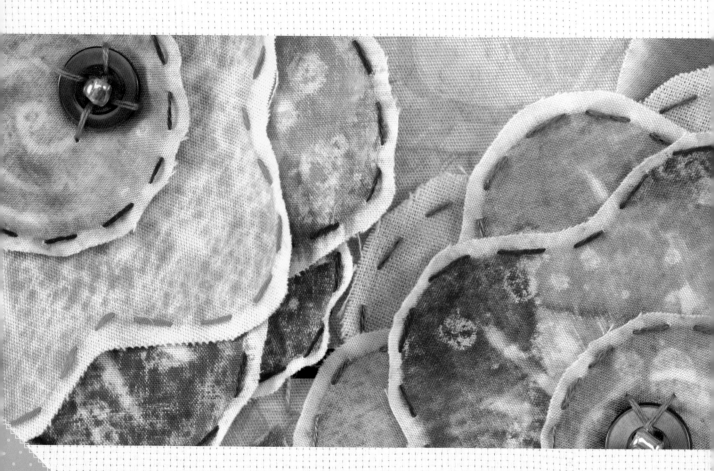

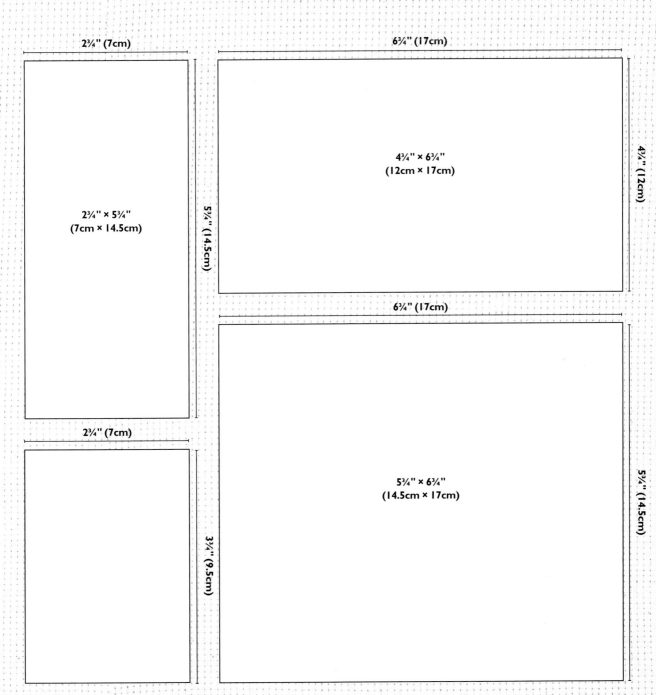

2¾" (7cm)

6¾" (17cm)

2¾" × 5¾"
(7cm × 14.5cm)

4¾" × 6¾"
(12cm × 17cm)

4¾" (12cm)

5¾" (14.5cm)

2¾" (7cm)

6¾" (17cm)

5¾" × 6¾"
(14.5cm × 17cm)

5¾" (14.5cm)

3¾" (9.5cm)

ASSEMBLING THE ART QUILT

materials

12 completed art quilt blocks

dowel rod or decorative branch

32 ⅜" (1cm) grommets

tools

grommet pliers

pencil

scissors

twine or ribbon

1 Arrange the quilt blocks in rows as desired. I arranged 3 rows of 4 to accommodate 12 quilt blocks. Play with the arrangement until it looks good to you.

2 Starting with the top left quilt block, trace the inside of a grommet to draw 2 holes at the top of the quilt with a pencil 1" (2.5cm) from the top and 3" (7.5cm) in on each side. Draw 2 more holes 1" (2.5cm) from the bottom and 3" (7.5cm) in on each side at the bottom of the quilt.

Displaying the Quilt

I designed this quilt to hang in three columns, but as a variation you could attach each row and each column of the quilt to create one large hanging. To display your quilt on a wall, thread ribbon or twine from the top grommets of each column and secure them on a dowel rod or decorative branch.

3 Punch a hole in the fabric with grommet pliers. (Use scissors if the fabric is difficult to cut.) Force a ⅜" (1cm) grommet into the hole from the right side of the fabric and place the washer right side up over the grommet post.

4 Position the grommet pliers over the grommet and washer and squeeze firmly to secure the grommet in the block. Repeat for the other side.

5 Continue the same process until all 12 blocks have grommets in them. All the blocks, except those in the last row, will need 4 grommets: 2 at the top and 2 at the bottom. The last row only needs 2 grommets at the top.

6 Cut 24 pieces of twine or ribbon 16" (40.5cm) long. Thread a piece through the bottom grommet hole of 1 quilt block, attaching it to the top grommet hole of the quilt block below it by tying in a double knot. Trim the edges and thread the knot through the grommet so it is hidden. Repeat this step for the grommets on the other side. Leave a 4" (10cm) space between each block.

THE DRESS
Kristen Feighery

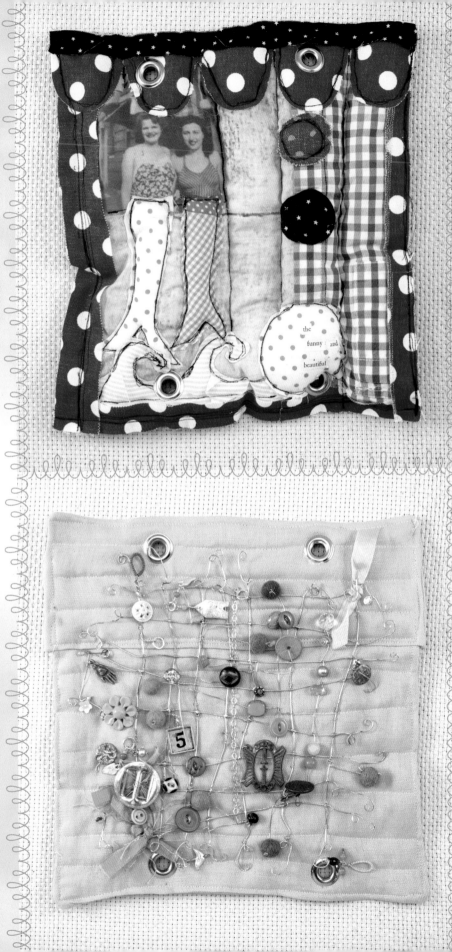

THE
FUNNY AND
BEAUTIFUL
SEA
Jenn McGlon

HARD WIRED
Catherine Thursby

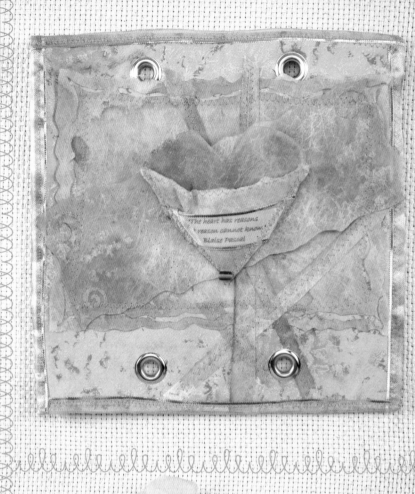

THE HEART HAS REASONS
Yetta Miller

GATHERED IN GRANDMOTHER'S GARDEN
Liz Lamoreux

MY
COLORFUL
SIDE
Chrissie Grace

TATTERED
PIECES
Sandy Mastroni

Resources and Information

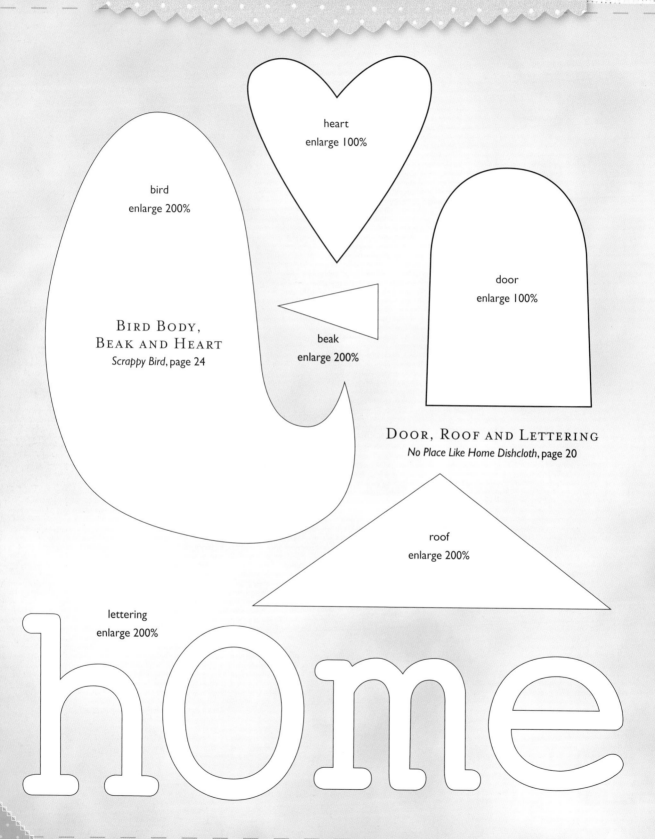

heart
enlarge 100%

bird
enlarge 200%

door
enlarge 100%

**BIRD BODY,
BEAK AND HEART**
Scrappy Bird, page 24

beak
enlarge 200%

DOOR, ROOF AND LETTERING
No Place Like Home Dishcloth, page 20

roof
enlarge 200%

lettering
enlarge 200%

home

PAGE BASE
Assembling the Journal, page 72

enlarge 125%

Danita Art is a self-taught mixed-media artist. She loves elephants and dogs. She makes her creations during the night, and she considers herself a night owl. Danita loves to work with different media. Her work has been featured in several publications, including *Somerset Studio*, *Stuffed*, *Belle Armoire* and *Art Doll Quarterly*.

Alisa Burke is a freelance painter and mixed-media artist. She studied fine art at Portland State University with a major in painting and printmaking. Alisa is always looking for new ways to break the rules and redefine art. She draws inspiration from street art, graffiti, art history and fashion, and it is not uncommon to find her digging through the trash in hopes of recycling something unique to use in her art work. Alisa's paintings have been exhibited in a variety of galleries, and her handmade, painted accessories are carried in a number of boutiques across the country. Her art work has been featured in publications such as *Cloth Paper Scissors*, *Haute Handbags*, *Art Doll Quarterly*, and the *USD Magazine*. Her first book, *Canvas Remix*, was released in spring of 2008.

Jessica Fediw is a crafty stay-at-home mom to one adorable little girl. She is also a wife to a Coastie. Jessica writes about her crafty endeavors on her blog (http://www.ohsohappytogether.blogspot.com) and also shares tutorials and life happenings. She loves to sew and crochet the most but is constantly trying to learn new things. She also has an Etsy shop (http://www.ohsohappytogether.etsy.com) where she posts things she creates and original sewing patterns.

Kristen Feighery is a rising artist on the Charlotte art scene. Her unique blend of modernism and folk art is rapidly gaining attention and winning her repeat buyers both locally and nationally.

Kristen grew up in Kentucky, deep in the Appalachian Mountains. She graduated from the liberal arts college of Christopher Newport University in Virginia with a degree in theatre arts and worked several years as a professional actress, touring with theatre companies up and down the East coast. In 2004, after taking a break from her career to become a mother, Kristen decided to pursue painting full-time. She incorporates everything into her work, from beeswax to bible pages, sheet music to wooden doors.

Kristen's work is featured at the gallery she owns and operates, Sanctuary of Davidson, and also at Atelier 24 Lexington in Ashville, NC.

Claudine Hellmuth is a nationally recognized collage artist, author and illustrator. She combines photos, paint, paper and pen into quirky, whimsical-retro collages that she calls Poppets.

Her art work has been featured on *The Martha Stewart Show*, in Mary Engelbreit's *Home Companion* magazine, *The New York Times*, on HGTV's *I Want That!* and on the DIY Network's *Craft Lab*.

In addition to creating her art work full-time, Claudine has developed a product line with Ranger Industries Inc. under the brand name of Claudine Hellmuth Studio, teaches collage workshops in the United States and Canada, and has written three books and made three DVDs about her techniques.

Originally from Orlando, Florida, Claudine now lives in Washington, DC with her husband Paul and their very spoiled cats, Mabel and Stanley.

Liz Lamoreux was ten when she began sewing as part of her summer involvment in the local 4H program. Although the other girls created mid-80s inspired mini skirts, she created a calico skirt and matching floral drawstring bag because she wanted to look like Laura Ingalls. During her teens, her creative focus was on writing and surrounding herself with books that became her best friends. After college, her soul-searching adventures transported her into the world of poetry, yoga and meditation. In the last few years, she has found herself drawn to the stories told by images from her childhood—vintage handkerchiefs, bowls of seashells, glass bottles and her grandmother's sewing basket. She can often be found in her studio, surrounded by strips of fabric, vintage buttons, several idea and poetry journals and a mug of tea. As a yoga teacher and artist, she sees creating as a meditative exercise for the spirit and is currently focusing on sharing this inward journey with others.

Sandy Mastroni is a self-taught artist who works in all forms of mixed media, from clay and acrylics to pen and ink, to create her three-dimensional works of art. She has been painting for over fifty years and paints crazy and wonderful images which are both thought-provoking and comical. She is inspired by music, other artists and creative forces. She paints ladies, cats, mermaids, fish, dogs and whimsical images of the moon. It doesn't take much to get her going on a piece once she is inspired. Her works are displayed in galleries across the country and are loved by many who have a great sense of humor or just love the beautiful images and unique vintage look.

Sandy lives in Connecticut with her husband and five cats.

Jenn McGlon, of Noodle and Lou Studio, is a self-taught artist living in the Chicago area with her husband and two boys. Noodle and Lou is named after the nicknames she had for her boys when they were born, Mr. Noodle and Little Lou. Jenn's work encompasses several different mediums and includes mixed-media paintings and a collection of polymer clay sculptures called "The Lulettes." Funky little couples, houses and girls with faraway looks in their eyes are her favorite things to create. Jenn's art is meant to make you smile and bring some fun into your home. Her works are collected around the world, which tickles and delights her to no end. Dreams really do come true . . . .

As a young girl, Yetta Miller was blessed to have a mother that loved to sew, knit, quilt and embroider. Her mother also loved that Yetta was an avid learner of all of the above. Yetta made her first sweater at nine years old and a lined suit at ten. Sewing, stitchery and knitting have always been a part of her life. During her undergraduate studies in art education, metal sculpture, clay and weaving were at the forefront for a time. While working towards her graduate degree in art therapy, she blended collage, papermaking, stained glass and mosaics with her sculpture, fabric and thread arts. She appreciates and is empowered by the melding of many mediums, especially when used with wonder for self-expression by both herself and her clients.

By training, Sara Mincy is a teacher and taught kindergarten for a number of years. By passion, however, she is an artist, and the world is her canvas! Even while teaching kindergarten, her friends would tease her that "everything she had her kids do became an art project." Today, Sara is privileged to homeschool her own children and concentrate on her art. She loves to paint canvases with whimsical images, patterns, scripture and inspirational quotes. Her goal is to communicate her faith in God through the artistic talent He has given her. Currently, she has a full line of prints and note cards and is working on her first children's book. In addition, she is in high demand as a commissioned artist and enjoys painting for other people and giving them art work that will make their lives more cozy, colorful and happy.

Ruth Rae is a classically trained jeweler. During her tenure as a metalsmith she began to experiment with other forms of media and techniques. As time progressed, Ruth's true passion became mixed-media fiber art. Ruth's pieces are recognized for their unexpected yet elegant combinations of altered fabrics combined with found objects and words that are bound together by hand and machine stitching. Ruth's work has been featured in galleries across the country and countless art publications, as well as Quilting Arts TV. She has also hosted two workshop DVDs. Ruth coauthored a unique jewelry book, *A Charming Exchange*, and her second book, *Layered, Tattered and Stitched: A Fabric Art Workshop*, was released in winter 2009.

Heather Sleightholm is a wife, mother and folk artist living in northeastern Oklahoma. Born and raised on the prairie, Heather graduated from Oklahoma State University and worked as a jewelry designer and then newspaper reporter before becoming a full-time mother. In the fall of 2007 she started her folk art business, Audrey Eclectic, named after her daughter. Today, Heather is constantly busy creating unique folk collage art, participating in local indie craft shows and raising her family. Find out more about Heather and her art at her Web site, www.audreyeclectic.com.

Catherine Thursby is a shop owner, mom, artist, wife and dog lover.

She has been creating since she was a child and works in a variety of media, from paints and fabrics to metals and vintage goods. She loves to mix the modern with the vintage and uses splashes of color when she can. Her work tends to be more on the fun, playful side of things, similar to her personality. She doesn't take things too seriously.

Catherine was born and raised in Michigan, where she lives with her husband, two children and her dog, Pearl. You can visit her online shop at www.redshoeshomegoods. com or her blog at www.redshoesllc. typepad.com.

Lori Vliegen works and plays in a happy place called Elvie Studio. Having been blessed with a very curious spirit of creativity, her art path has taken her just about everywhere, using just about every medium available. Lori discovered a true passion for letterforms early in life and has spent the past twenty years studying the fine art of calligraphy. She loves finding new ways to incorporate her letterforms into different projects, and has used materials such as paper, glass, metal, fabric, ceramics, clay and vinyl. Her art work has been seen in many different museums and venues, and she has been honored to particpate in two juried exhibits at the Smithsonian National Postal Museum. Enjoying life in northern Florida, Lori and her husband Walter have two wonderful children and a sweet bearded collie named Molly. Please visit Lori at her blog (www.elviestudio. blogspot.com) and her Etsy store (www.elviestudio.etsy.com).

Sarah Wyman is a mixed-media collage artist living in St. Louis, Missouri. She is married, the proud mama of two young children and is also near completion of a BFA in Art Education. She is an all-inclusive artist and has never met a craft she didn't like.

Sarah mainly creates female figurative work in collage, using bits and pieces from her flea-market finds. Her favorite materials include antique atlases, old wood letters as stamps and vintage magazines. She works with acrylic, pencil, ink, charcoal and paper to capture the unique expressions of her ladies.

Sarah started selling her original paintings and mixed-media pieces on eBay over four years ago and just recently expanded to Etsy. Her work can be found at http://sarah-greenweeds.blogspot.com, which has links to her eBay and Etsy shops. You can contact Sarah at seesew333@gmail.com.

ABOUT THE AUTHOR

Chrissie Grace is a mixed-media artist and the author of two other books, *Wild Tiles* and *Tiles Gone Wild*, both published by North Light Books. In addition to being a full-time mom, she is a also a full-time artist.

Chrissie's work focuses on the whimsical and colorful aspects of life and shows the expansion of her creativity and her need to test limits. Her work centers around inspirational themes and she loves to play with texture and substance. Chrissie enjoys experimenting with mosaics, mixed-media paintings, sewing and quilting, collage, photography and sculpture.

Chrissie lives and works just outside of Orlando, Florida, with her lovely family. For daily inspiration and to see more of Chrissie's work, check out her blog at www.chrissiegrace. blogspot.com.

RESOURCES

MODERN FABRICS

I believe strongly in supporting your local fabric stores. Selecting fabrics in person also gives you a much clearer idea of the true color and quality of the fabrics. However, shopping for fabric online is also a fun option.

Currently, my favorite brands of fabric are:

Alexander Henry Fabrics, Inc.
www.ahfabrics.com

Amy Butler
www.amybutlerdesign.com

Anna Maria
www.annamariahorner.com

**Claudine Hellmuth
Sticky-Back Canvas**
www.collageartist.com
www.rangerink.com

Heather Ross
www.heatherrossdesigns.com

Joel Dewberry
www.joeldewberry.com

Kaffee Fassett Studio
www.kaffefassett.com

Michael Miller Fabrics LLC
www.michaelmillerfabrics.com

Moda
www.unitednotions.com

Robert Kaufman Fabrics
www.robertkaufman.com

VINTAGE FABRICS

Vintage fabrics are used often in this book. You may have your own collection, but if not, they are pretty easy to find. Try thrift stores, garage sales and flea markets; Ebay (www.ebay.com) is a great online option.

OTHER SUPPLIES

CUTTING MATS, RULERS, SCISSORS, AND ROTARY CUTTERS

Fiskars
www.fiskars.com

Olfa
www.olfa.com

FABRIC PAINT

Plaid
www.plaidonline.com

Jacquard
www.jacquardproducts.com

INDEX

create and share with North Light books

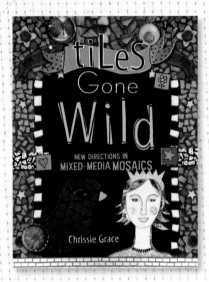

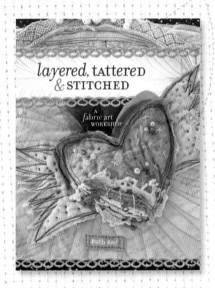

TILES GONE WILD

NEW DIRECTIONS IN MIXED-MEDIA MOSAICS

Chrissie Grace

Chrissie Grace, author of the best-selling *Wild Tiles*, will send your mosaic work in new directions with *Tiles Gone Wild*. You'll learn how to combine traditional, commercial tile with handmade clay tiles, crushed glass, stained glass and mixed-media elements in twenty whimsical step-by-step projects. Create fun and functional pieces for your home, patio and garden on unusual surfaces like PVC pipes and brick pavers. You'll even learn how to use photo-editing software to design personalized tile portraits.

ISBN-10: 1-60061-1081-1
ISBN-13: 978-1-60061-1081-3
paperback, 8.25" × 10.875", 128 pages
Z1929

LAYERED, TATTERED AND STITCHED

A FABRIC ART WORKSHOP

Ruth Rae

The step-by-step instructions found in *Layered, Tattered and Stitched* will provide you with the inspiration and techniques in order to create fabric art with incredible depth and personal signifcance. Throughout the book, the author uses a mixture of atypical sewing techniques such as trapping found objects between layers, stitching and quilting paper, and creating windows in fabric along with mixed-media techniques that include transferring photos, staining fabric, and more to create magnificent works of art. Expand your creative process, using such things as poetry and symbolic objects for inspiration.

ISBN-10: 1-60061-188-5
ISBN-13: 978-1-60061-188-9
paperback, 8.25" × 10.875", 128 pages
Z2783

CREATIVE BLOOM

PROJECTS AND INSPIRATION WITH FABRIC AND WIRE

Jennifer Swift

Creative Bloom combines two diverse materials—fabric and wire—to instruct you on how to create décor items such as photo holders, sun-catchers, garlands, ornaments, a lamp, a bird sculpture, and even a few jewelry pieces. All projects and techniques in the book are centered around shaping wire and combining it with assorted fabrics while enhancing pieces with embellishments and handstitching. You will be inspired to bring creativity into you daily life with chapters focusing on different approaches to the creative process.

ISBN-10: 1-4403-0316-9
ISBN-13: 978-1-4403-0316-6
paperback, 8.25" × 10.875", 128 pages
Z6943

144